"María Ruiz Scaperlanda's intimate p
Nyirumbe in *Sewing Hope in Uganda* delights the reader with rich
details and tender observations that reveal a complex woman of
God who can be fierce yet gentle, tenacious and bold, unrelenting
but loving. Scaperlanda's masterful storytelling invites us on a
journey of discovery into the heart of Sr. Rosemary's mission to
empower women devastated by violence and oppression in Uganda."

—Maria Morera Johnson, author of *Super Girls and Halos:
My Companions on the Quest for Truth, Justice and
Heroic Virtue* and *My Badass Book of Saints:
Courageous Women Who Showed Me How to Live*

"This small book is a moving introduction to the life and work of
Sister Rosemary Nyirumbe who has been called the 'Mother Teresa
of Africa'. Be prepared to be inspired by the joy, the faith, the
motherly love and indomitable spirit of this woman who has had
such impact in the lives of young African women and girls who
were victims of one of the most horrific atrocities of our time. It is
a testament to hope and healing."

—Most Reverend Paul S. Coakley
Archbishop of Oklahoma City

"Where there is great evil, there is often greater good to be found,
if we could only see it. Maria Scaperlanda's moving account of
Sister Rosemary Nyirumbe's work in Uganda is a powerful
testament to a diminutive Sister with the heart of a lioness. Sister
Rosemary has faced down great evil with greater faith while
rescuing the victims of one of Africa's most cruel conflicts.
Rosemary Nyirumbe: Sewing Hope in Uganda is a story of hope
for all Christians and a moving testimony to the witness of the
Church in East Africa, a modern-day cradle of martyrs and saints-
in-the-making."

—Greg Erlandson, Director and Editor in Chief, Catholic
News Service

People of God

Remarkable Lives, Heroes of Faith

People of God is a series of inspiring biographies for the general reader. Each volume offers a compelling and honest narrative of the life of an important twentieth- or twenty-first-century Catholic. Some living and some now deceased, each of these women and men has known challenges and weaknesses familiar to most of us but responded to them in ways that call us to our own forms of heroism. Each offers a credible and concrete witness of faith, hope, and love to people of our own day.

Rosemary Nyirumbe

Sewing Hope in Uganda

María Ruiz Scaperlanda

LITURGICAL PRESS
Collegeville, Minnesota

www.litpress.org

Cover design by Red+Company. Cover illustration by Philip Bannister.

Excerpt from the English translation of Non-Biblical Readings from *The Liturgy of the Hours* © 1973, 1974, 1975, International Commission on English in the Liturgy Corporation (ICEL). All rights reserved.

Excerpts from Pope Francis's *Gaudete et Exsultate* © Libreria Editrice Vaticana. Used with permission.

1   2   3   4   5   6   7   8   9

Library of Congress Control Number: 2018952112

ISBN 978-0-8146-4463-8   978-0-8146-4486-7 (e-book)

*To the Sisters of the Sacred Heart of Jesus
in Uganda, Kenya, and South Sudan,
and to all unknown or forgotten women
who have transformed families, communities,
and countries
by the power of their faith witness*

Contents

Foreword

The Hasidic rabbi Levi Yitzhak of the Ukraine is fond of telling friends of his visit to the Polish countryside. One evening the rabbi was visiting the owner of a tavern. As he walked in, he saw two peasants at a table. Both were drinking with reckless abandon, arms around each other, protesting how much each loved the other. Suddenly Ivan said to Peter: "Peter, tell me, what hurts me?" Bleary-eyed, Peter looked at Ivan: "How do I know what hurts you?" Ivan's answer was swift: "If you don't know what hurts me, how can you say you love me?"

Like Ivan, my good friend Sister Rosemary Nyirumbe believes she needs to know all the afflictions of the youth she serves with a heart akin to the master Jesus. Sister Rosemary listens with attentive love to everyone she ministers to, but there is obviously a special place in her heart for the girls at St. Monica's Girls Tailoring Center in Gulu, Uganda. She helps them to reclaim their lives from their former rebel captors.

The girls Sister Rosemary ministers to are among the most stigmatized of all youth. They regularly encounter cruel remarks within their home communities that make them grow more and more bitter: "You are carrying the child of a murderer." "You are damaged goods." "You are a disgrace to your family and to all of us." Sister Rosemary has set her heart on healing the wounds of this war. She is starting by healing the wounded spirits of these child mothers who lost so much of their self-esteem to the nightmarish disaster in their homeland. This determined nun has given hundreds upon hundreds of these girls vocational skills, an income, and taught them the techniques and know-how that will enable them to be self-sufficient in the future. The stories of pain and resilience found on these pages reveal an incredibly wise and prudent companion for humanity's young.

I could never forget my first experience with Sister Rosemary. In July of 2001, I journeyed from Kampala, Uganda, northward to Gulu. In those days, the roads were in deplorable condition and it was going to be a long day's trip. Still, Sister Rosemary insisted we carve out time to stop at a refugee camp we would pass by in order to spend time encouraging the vast throng of people who were forced to live there temporarily in dehumanizing squalor. We had no supplies or financial resources to share with these desperately deprived people. Nevertheless, Sister Rosemary had a word of encouragement for everyone she encountered, rallying hope in their spirits and spreading her infectious joy everywhere. Most of us would have been frightened or overwhelmed by such abject misery. Sister Rosemary saw an opportunity to bring Christ's compassionate spirit to humanity's most forgotten. I will never forget what I saw that day. I will never again underestimate the power of presence, companioning others who have been forced to bear the most crushing burdens in the human family.

María Ruiz Scaperlanda has chronicled Sister Rosemary's life and ministry in a compelling narrative that will connect you to an extraordinary life well lived. Learning of the adventures of others who are reaching out to touch our hurting world with grace is a call to action for ourselves and all. It spurs us on to do whatever is in our power to allow the compassion of Jesus's spirit to flow through us.

On her trips abroad, Sister Rosemary always takes with her the beautiful craftwork of her girls to show to others and to sell on their behalf. This is one concrete measure that reinforces for the girls that they can make something valuable others will want and will help them generate income. The items that are most popular are necklaces made from discarded paper. It is rolled very, very tightly into beads, which are then dyed multicolors and strung together. The materials for crafting these necklaces cost practically nothing but the task is labor intensive. The final outcome is a gorgeous piece of jewelry that originates from discarded material. One woman who purchased a necklace while Sister Rosemary was visiting Cleveland, Ohio, relates how, several times a day while wearing that particularly precious necklace, she lets her fingers move gently across the beads. She pauses for a moment. That moment becomes a prayer as she calls to mind the girls who crafted this treasure and she asks God to favor their future with grace and goodness. By such simple acts of grace I see Sister Rosemary bringing our world together in realms of grace and friendship.

To many of us in North America, the senseless violence that Sister Rosemary has been an eyewitness of appears exceedingly tragic but remote. It must be the concern of someone other than ourselves. The moral genius of people like Sister Rosemary Nyirumbe is that they are teaching all of us that there is no such thing as other people's children. Whenever we allow a girl or boy anywhere on earth to be reduced to a nonperson, then one more thread is plucked out of the fabric that holds the human family together. Until our moral outrage joins with Sister Rosemary's and that of our brothers and sisters around the world, children will continue to suffer in hidden ways.

Where others see only pain, danger, and a reason why they are unable to act, Sister Rosemary sees possibilities and promise. If I were restricted to a single adjective to describe Sister Rosemary, I know what word I would choose. Courageous! On a Sunday afternoon enjoying lunch with the nuns at St. Monica's, I was caught up in yet another courageous episode along Sister Rosemary's journey. A dozen girls raced into the dining hall screaming for help and shouting about a cobra in the henhouse. There was a ten-foot-long, deadly cobra that had made its way onto the school property. I immediately jumped up and went looking for a custodian, or some other brave staff member, to confront this lethal danger. Sister Rosemary immediately jumped up and went for a machete, which she could use to attack the cobra and defend the girls. I watched, from a safe distance, as Sister Rosemary attacked the cobra, cutting it in ten pieces! The girls had long known that Sister Rosemary would do anything to defend them. This was one more proof of a commitment that is helping to heal and transform their lives.

Michael Ford, in his biography of the Dutch theologian Henri Nouwen, tells us how radically honest Nouwen was emotionally. Sometimes when loneliness or suffering would threaten to overwhelm him, Nouwen would go to a friend's house and ask that friend to hold him while he cried. Not an easy thing to do, but in it there is a lesson: when we stare life's pain and our own fears fully in the face, someone or something had better be holding us or that darkness will destroy us rather than make us stronger.

Sister Rosemary has spent a lifetime holding in her arms the hurting children of Africa. Her inspiration can be a guidepost for us all! The moving stories told here by María Ruiz

Scaperlanda are certain to inspire compassionate action and greater solidarity. Faith requires no less of a response.

Rev. Donald H. Dunson, PhD
Author of *No Room at the Table:*
Earth's Most Vulnerable Children and
Child, Victim, Soldier: The Loss of Innocence in Uganda

Acknowledgments

It is difficult to express just what a pleasure it has been to write about Sister Rosemary Nyirumbe, to be the author who has the privilege of introducing this formidable woman to the readers of the People of God series.

Over the past several decades I have been privileged to meet and write about many impressive Catholics from around the world. Sometimes they are well known, even famous—men and women who are impressive in their dedication and generous spirit, as well as worthy of our admiration and respect.

Yet what has been most rewarding for me over the years as a Catholic journalist is to find those souls who toil away—almost always unknown and unrecognized—who are living faith-filled, prayer-full lives, and who are consistent in living their Catholic faith. Paraphrasing Cardinal Joseph Bernardin's words, each of these men and women embodies what it means to be a Catholic wrapped in a seamless garment of faith. Truly, something inside me leaps every time I encounter them, the Holy Spirit rejoicing and recognizing the Truth and Love lived by these individuals.

Sister Rosemary Nyirumbe is one such spirit, someone both Orthodox and radical. Yes, she is a woman of deep faith, grounded in the Eucharist, and a Sister of the Sacred

Heart of Jesus community. But as she likes to say, don't dismiss her struggle because she is a nun!

Sister Rosemary is a genuine disciple of Jesus Christ because she chooses to grapple daily with what it means to live out her vocation—especially reaching out to the broken and bleeding and needy, the living Body of Christ whom she sees in the women and orphans in northern Uganda. It is her ministry of presence, above all, that makes her example so powerful and meaningful.

My first thanks, therefore, is to Barry Hudock, who invited me to take on this beautiful project. Also, many thanks to the Liturgical Press staff who have worked with me at every step of the publishing process to bring this book into your hands.

It has been my heart's pleasure to meet the community of the Sacred Heart of Jesus in Uganda. Thank you for your generous hospitality, for bringing us into your prayer and sharing with us your every meal. You made me feel so at home! A special thank-you to Sister Doreen Oyella and to Comboni Father Luigi Gabaglio, who so generously traveled many hours and many days throughout northern Uganda with us, always willing, explaining, remembering, and introducing me to their world.

This book owes a great debt to Reggie Whitten, and to the Sewing Hope Foundation and Pros for Africa, for introducing us to Sister Rosemary through the book *Sewing Hope,* and to Derek Watson and his brilliant staff at Lighthouse Media for their award-winning documentary by the same name. I hope and pray that this book makes everyone who reads it want to know more. I heartily recommend readers to visit SewingHopeFoundation.com to learn how to join Sister Rosemary in her ministry.

How can I thank my sister in faith and heart friend, Sister Rosemary, whose voice I regularly hear in my head, singing to me, "María . . . makes me . . . laugh!" May God bless abundantly your willing heart. Thank you for your witness of faith and service, for your generous love, for bringing me into your expansive heart—and for showing me what it means to recognize God in every person and every situation. You continue to inspire me!

Finally, as always, I'd like to express my gratitude to the Tribe that is my family—my mother and brother, my adult children, my amazing Grands, and especially my husband, Michael, for his encouragement and love, and for introducing me to Sister Rosemary!

Introduction

A sad nun is a bad nun. . . . I am more afraid of
one unhappy sister than a crowd of evil spirits. . . .
What would happen if we hid what little sense of
humor we had? Let each of us humbly use this to
cheer others.

> Teresa of Ávila, in James Martin, SJ,
> *Between Heaven and Mirth*

Our four-wheeling Toyota Land Cruiser snakes and curves
in the twilight, struggling to miss as many potholes as possible. But some dirt holes are simply so large that they bring
our vehicle to a complete stop before our skilled driver can
finally, slowly, move us forward.

Fast or slow, red dirt rises around us like a thick fog,
restraining our vision and overpowering our sense of smell.
Shockingly, neither the darkness nor the dirt, not even our
speed, impedes pedestrians of all ages from sharing the road
with us.

I watch a line of three women, one behind the other, carrying five-gallon yellow containers of water on their heads.
Even as our car slides past them, the women continue, seem-
ingly unaffected, determined, skillfully maneuvering their own
steps around both the fast-moving vehicles and potholes.

We are in northern Uganda, in what is colloquially known as West Nile, a mere stone's throw away from the South Sudan border. I'm sharing the back seat of the four-wheel-drive vehicle with Sister Rosemary Nyirumbe, who nudges me, then raises her hand to point to the sign rushing past us, announcing our destination: Moyo. It's no wonder that she warned me as we got in the car, "The road to Moyo is like going to Calvary! But Moyo . . . Moyo is paradise!"

Much like the way that New York City locals describe distance in time, not miles, Sister Rosemary's eyes smile as she turns and whispers to me, "Only twenty more minutes," which in non-Uganda time *really* means at least another half hour, although not quite an hour. No matter. She continues fidgeting with the beads of her rosary with her left hand. In map terms, we are a mere ninety-one miles northwest of Gulu, the largest city in northern Uganda, but the journey has already taken several hours.

The landscape surrounding us is anything but an urban metropolis. It smells humid, and it is eerily silent. The car headlights bounce light into the growing darkness, occasionally revealing a goat in the bush or a group of barefooted children herding a cow with a stick on their way home for supper. We are slowly climbing up, with mahogany trees and luscious bush showing off their beauty to either side of us.

In modern African history, northern Uganda is infamously known for its violent stories. Idi Amin carried out mass executions of its native Acholi and Lango Christian tribes as well as other ethnic groups, a tragedy followed by years of tribal "bush wars." Soon afterward, for decades that persisted into the early 2000s, the region sheltered the violent guerrillas of warlord Joseph Rao Kony and his militia, the Lord's Resistance Army (LRA), as it moved across the borders of Sudan, Congo, and back.

Hearing the stories of Sister Rosemary Nyirumbe's life makes the history of northern Uganda seem simultaneously otherworldly and intensely relevant. Her story is, in fact, intricately woven with the tragic, extreme, yet ultimately hopeful history of this region in central Africa.

Best known as the driving force who saved hundreds of children from abduction during the bloody wars that have devastated northern Uganda and Sudan for decades, Sister Rosemary walks with a sense and force of purpose and, always, with joy. No small task for a woman who not only lived through these often brutal moments in her country's history, but who also stood up to the evil before her, time and time again—all in the name of what she calls the gospel of presence, healing, and forgiveness.

She was born in Paidha, approximately one hundred miles—but four and a half hours by car—southwest of Moyo. For almost twenty years, she has lived and worked at St. Monica's Girls Tailoring Centre rescuing and teaching marketable skills to women and children who suffered first when they were abducted, and then again when they were forced to join the violent, gruesome world of Kony's militia. The one place that has always welcomed them back from the bush is St. Monica's in Gulu, 122 miles and over three hours on dirt roads from the small village of huts with grass roofs where she was born. As she likes to note, she has spent almost all of the sixty-two years of her life living in basically three locations, which form a triangle in northern Uganda: Paidha, Moyo, and Gulu—strategically situated on the main route between the capital cities of Kampala (Uganda) and Juba (South Sudan).

Perhaps that's part of what makes Sister Rosemary's recent world-wide notoriety all the more remarkable. While she doesn't hesitate to speak out for the poorest among us, she nevertheless shies away from recognition—quickly pointing to others in her community and to the brave work they are doing. She laughs often, and heartily, especially as she explains how most members of her tribe, the Alur, look physically like her—"short and robust"—while their neighbors, the Acholi, are lean and tall. Yet the same woman who jokes about her five-foot stature has also shaken hands with foreign presidents, kings, American NBA stars, and Pope Francis. Rome Reports described her in 2017 as "the Mother Teresa of Africa." But, she will interrupt to say, grinning, "None of these things make me taller than what I am! I'm level headed because I don't see these things as lifting me to be someone different."

Although active abductions of children in northern Uganda ended in 2006, even now the girls are continuing to escape from their bush captivity. And Sister Rosemary passionately describes story after horrifying story of what these children have lived through and why they need us. "Just last year we had girls who came to us from captivity. This year we have two girls who were BORN in captivity!" While the sisters' work has changed, she emphasizes, it is far from done—remaining faithful to the mission of providing a safe home and education for victims of war and violence, particularly orphans and young women.

If her eyes could talk, they would tell hundreds of gruesome stories that Sister Rosemary has witnessed or heard throughout the years—like the story of Valerie,[1] the girl who arrived at St. Monica's with a baby barely a month old. After years in the bush under rebels' rule, Valerie had escaped, just one week after giving birth to little Joy. When Valerie approached Sister Rosemary grumbling about her roommate, Sister Rosemary initially dismissed it as a petty grievance between girls. Then Valerie began to describe how the rebels had forced her to kill villagers "in the most brutal way"—including her roommate's parents. "Now she is helping me take care of my baby," she told Sister Rosemary. "I feel so bad . . . I can't sleep in the same room with her. What if she finds out?" As Valerie sobbed, Sister Rosemary pondered how to be a mother in this terrible situation.

"Don't be afraid," Sister Rosemary finally said to Valerie. "Tell her what happened. She may be upset at first, but she will understand because she was forced to do the same to other people. So she knows what it's like, and she will eventually forgive you. . . . You are sisters now." Loving those who have never known love—and whom the world believes don't deserve love, notes Sister Rosemary—required that she and her sisters become spiritual mothers for the girls at St. Monica's. And that's exactly what the Sisters of the Sacred Heart of Jesus have done in Gulu, for the past two decades.

Sister Rosemary Nyirumbe is one of *Time* magazine's "100 Most Influential People in the World" (2014). She is the subject of the book *Sewing Hope* and a documentary by the same name, narrated by Academy Award–winning actor Forest Whitaker (2013). She received the United Nations Impact Award, the John Paul II *Veritatis Splendor* Award, and she has been named a CNN Hero. She even had a song written in her honor, "Touched by a Rose," by JAIA.

But for "baby sister," as her brothers, sisters, and family still call her, speaking engagements and awards are simply occasions to tell the story, "platforms where I can really speak on behalf of the voiceless, where I can speak perhaps a little louder than I could if I was only there. That's all!" She pauses, smiles. "I have the great opportunity to speak on behalf of people who cannot speak for themselves."

The truth is that "I am not strong," says Sister Rosemary surprisingly, before adding, "so that keeps me dependent on

God! I keep praying, '*Give me the energy and the strength, and give me the right words to speak to each audience.*'" She looks to fellow Catholics for leadership in promoting the Gospel with compassion and justice, even though, she acknowledges, "oftentimes Catholics don't show their faith easily. But you can't sugarcoat evil. It would be better for us to begin to show our faith better. I would like the Catholics to continue being leaders. We have to speak up a little more!"—especially when it comes to being present to our suffering brothers and sisters around the globe.

Her eyes smile as she answers questions about her prayer life, noting that she loves the rosary. She has prayed the same four-word supplication every day of her life, "*Rwoth para, Mungu para*, my Lord and my God"—always spoken in her soul-language of Alur. "Love is the key for doing all the work we can do," she clarifies, adding that Mother Teresa has joined her personal posse of saints, the ones that she relies on, because Mother Teresa's calling was to do small things with great love. "Real love will *always* make you different."

Sister Rosemary credits her love of children and the Italian Comboni sisters for her passionate ministry and religious vocation, a call she answered at the young age of fifteen. Her community of over 325 sisters, in fact, grew out of the Comboni Missionaries, when in 1976 the Comboni sisters encouraged them to form their own African community and to elect their first African superior general. In addition to their motherhouse in Juba, South Sudan, the Sacred Heart of Jesus Sisters also live out their motto—"Live Love in Truth"—in Kenya and Uganda, where most Sacred Heart vocations come from.

* * *

As our white Toyota approaches the gray and white Moyo Redeemer Orphanage building where we're going to spend the night, a weary Sister Rosemary leads us to an entryway with words painted in blue below a brick archway, "THIS HOME WAS FUNDED BY INTERNATIONAL REFUGEE TRUST-LONDON (IRT)." But before any one of us can say or do anything, we hear them. A lively group of girls wearing their finest dresses and boys in their best collar shirts begin singing a lovely welcome to us.

In spite of the late hour and her own tiredness, Sister Rosemary stops, leans against the wall, and begins clapping to the beat, letting the kids know that she loves it. She is beaming. The tune changes, the clapping continues, and a small girl walks forward, hands Sister a small flower, and curtsies away, too shy to stay long. But when the music stops, children of all ages reach out to touch the motherly sister whose hugs and voice embody God's love for each of them.

The older kids, who have been standing back behind the singers, patiently wait for their own moment with "Sister." She may be exhausted from the day of travel, but her demeanor, voice, and intensity do not show it. Sister Rosemary quizzes three of the taller girls on their current school subjects, then brings the conversation to a close by asking them, "What time are lights out? Shouldn't you already be in bed?" The girls just giggle in reply, wandering down the hall, presumably to their dormitory.

This Moyo orphanage has a lot of history, and a lot of stories to tell. But they will wait until the morning. Our group of five washes up, then sits to eat a banquet of grains, beans, vegetables with peanut sauce, fresh fruits, and *kwen*, also known as *kwon* in Acholi, a doughlike brown food served often with a meal. No salt-dried crickets tonight—a delicacy of northern Uganda, and a favorite treat of Sister Rosemary's.

Even at this late hour, Sister Rosemary has a remarkable, spontaneous sense of humor. When I ask her to turn to Sister Doreen for a staged photo, the two sisters start talking in Arabic and laughing out loud. Afterward she confesses, "We know not very useful Arabic!" she laughs. "I asked her, 'Are you drunk?' And Sister Doreen said, 'No, I'm not drunk!'"

But the memories of Sister Rosemary's time here are bittersweet, at best. Tribal conflicts. Soldiers and rebels. Children caught in the middle of the violence, sometimes abandoned by their own terrified parents fleeing the bloodshed. Little food. Delivering babies by flashlight in nighttime so dark that at times you can't see your hand in front of your face.

Every retelling, however, concludes with a story about a particular child that she always remembers by name. And in almost every case, Sister Rosemary can add an epilogue to the trauma suffered by that child, one that makes it clear that she never stops touching base with the children in her stories, no matter how much time has passed by.

On my way to our bedroom, where we'll sleep one night before heading to the Sacred Heart Sisters Ugandan Motherhouse on the other side of Moyo, I walk past a sign marking,

> Inauguration
> Redeemer Children's Home
> 29th March 2007
> by H. G. (His Grace) Archbishop
> Christopher Pierre
> Apostolic Nuncio to Uganda

Which gives me even more questions for Sister Rosemary. But I know she will take her time and make all things clear to me, with patience, laughter, and joy, tomorrow—no matter how grim or difficult the tale that goes with the explanation. She is a woman of faith, and prayer obviously fuels Sister Rosemary's every effort.

Like Martin de Porres, Marianne Cope, and other saints who advocated for the oppressed, Sister Rosemary knows her own talents—and her own weaknesses. She acknowledges that she's not strong, not able to do what she has to do, what she knows she must do. But that's what has made her kneel before Jesus over and over again, like the Canaanite woman, boldly and full of certainty that her request will be answered. With her whole being, she lives her vocation to the least in her midst—the children, the girls no one wants, the babies that have been cast away, left behind.

My starting—and final—prayer for you, the reader, is one that I know I share with Sister Rosemary Nyirumbe's heart. May the stories you find here bring you closer to the heart of Jesus, and to Our Lady. In the words of Sister Rosemary, "It's good for me to be close to the Mother of Jesus. It keeps it all among women!"

Pray for us, o Holy Mother of God,
that we may be made worthy of the promises of Christ.
June 3, 2018
Feast of the Uganda martyrs

CHAPTER ONE

Little Sister's Beginnings
(1956–1975)

> This abandonment establishes the soul in a peace
> which renders her capable of facing all her troubles.
> . . . My soul made frequent acts of abandonment
> during these storms and ended them, this time, by
> the desire and resolution to do something more for
> God.
>
> Lucie Christine, in Astrid M. O'Brien, *A Mysticism
> of Kindness: The Biography of Lucie Christine*

Clumps of tall bushy pine trees seem out of place in the tropical highlands of northwest Uganda where nature shows off its bounty of cassava, coffee, mango, and banana trees. "They are grown for firewood," Sister Rosemary says, explaining how the pine trees came to be part of her familiar landscape overlooking the Western Rift Valley. This area connects to the African Great Lakes, including to the far south Lake Victoria, the second largest freshwater lake in the world (by area).

The closer one gets to Sister Rosemary's hometown of Paidha, on the West Nile, the more obvious the road walkers become. Men, women, children—all walk on both sides of the red dirt road leading into town, many of them preschool and grade school children wearing school uniforms. "Little kids like to go to school because they get breakfast!" Sister Rosemary says with a smile, unable to contain the excitement in her voice. This is home. On the edge of Paidha, and not far down the dirt road from the parish church, is where Rosemary Nyirumbe was born and raised—and a number of her relatives still reside. In the middle of town there's a statute of a leopard, a symbol of the Alur chiefdom. "There are a lot of beautiful things about this area that I didn't notice until I missed them," says Sister Rosemary, who was born here in 1956, "like the coolness of the air, the beauty of the Rift Valley, and the market. This village is now my favorite place to visit. It's hard to leave home."

Since 1997, the government-run education system in Uganda has been known as "Universal Primary Education," providing free education for children until the age of nineteen. But it is different for girls, notes Sister Rosemary. Parents with girls often keep them home to marry, and if a girl becomes pregnant she cannot go back to school. According to census data from 2004, for every ten students enrolled in primary schools, only one is enrolled at a secondary institution.[1] Officially, the literacy rate of Uganda is 69 percent, 76 percent for men, and 63 percent for women.[2]

But even sixty years ago, Ugandan education was better than that of their neighboring countries. And education was, in fact, the reason that Sister Rosemary's parents moved from their small town of Mahagi in Congo to Paidha, on the Uganda side of the banana trees. Martino Orwodhi and his wife Sabina Otiti had their first five children in Congo, and three more after crossing into Uganda, where their eight children grew up learning English—the official language of the state, due to the country's long history under British rule. "We were supposed to be nine," Sister Rosemary notes, "but one died [the second baby], Emilio. I never knew him." The sons in the family are four: Valerio, Thomas, Luigi, and Santos. But their dad, Martino, had a special place in his heart for his daughters: Martha, Catherine, Perpetua, and especially his baby girl, Rosemary.

Martha, Sister Rosemary's oldest sister, still lives in their mother's house in the small village of round huts with grass roofs where Rosemary was born and raised. "I grew up in a hut," Sister Rosemary says, looking over at the buildings shaped in a circle and clumped together. "The roofs are made of grass to keep the hut cooler," Sister Rosemary explains, noting that grass roofs last about five years. One family normally has several huts, using each one for different groups of members of the family, such as one for the older children and one for the parents with the youngest children. "Sometimes we'd wash clothes and lay them on the roof to dry," remembers Sister Rosemary. Their small grouping of homes is located so close to the Democratic Republic of the Congo (DRC) that DRC children cross the border regularly to attend school in their neighboring country. Sister Rosemary's childhood home is 122 miles and over three hours on a combination of tarmac and dirt roads from Gulu, where she now lives.

Unlike the typical cultural and historical distinctions made between men and women, Martino and Sabina valued education for their four boys *and* their four girls. Both sexes were also expected to toil in the garden ("woman's work") as well as learn basic wood workshop skills from their carpenter father. Even when other family members derided them for wasting time, money, and energy on their girls,

Sabina was determined to educate the children equally—and she regularly convinced her husband to agree.

In spite of having little money and no extras in her up-bringing, Rosemary grew up feeling happy and loved. From a very young age, she was quick to learn, a natural leader with the other children, and an excellent athlete—no doubt an acquired skill from years of keeping up with her older brothers. "I have many cousins and other relatives still living here," says Sister Rosemary with a smile. "They all call me baby sister."

Rosemary and her family come from the Alur people, part of the Lwo group, and their language is closely related to Acholi. According to Alur tradition, their people migrated from southern Sudan with other Lwo, following the banks of the Nile River into modern-day Uganda. Although also present in South Sudan, Kenya, Tanzania, and Congo, the large Lwo group lives mostly in the northern part of Uganda. Most members of the Alur tribe, in particular, reside in northern Uganda and far northeastern Congo. As much as they valued education, Sister Rosemary's parents would be proud to know that as an adult their youngest daughter speaks at least six languages.

When Rosemary was five years old, her parents packed up her things and took Rosemary across town to live with their oldest child, Martha, who was newly married. Although this type of arrangement is not part of Ugandan culture, it appears that it made sense for their family. Martha treated Rosemary like her first child, and in many ways, Rosemary regarded her oldest sister as another mother. About a year after Rosemary went to live with her, Martha gave birth to the first of her eight children. So as Rosemary grew older, she naturally learned parenting skills and sharpened her intrinsic maternal instinct while helping to care for her nieces and nephews.

In a very practical way, this upbringing helped Rosemary develop and cultivate the mothering spirit that has become the marker of Sister Rosemary's religious vocation and ministry. In fact, she believes that taking care of Martha's children also helped her discern her vocation. "I felt I really developed a connection with my nieces and nephews, and that was all that really became a part of my life. When I heard about sisters who came from Sudan and made their ministry caring for children and orphans, I felt it was the right place for me to be."

Perhaps the hardest thing for Rosemary to get used to when she moved out of her parents' house was adjusting to sleeping without siblings in the same hut. She took care of this by talking to herself at night, affirming herself over and over, "Yes, I can do this." During the time she lived with Martha, Rosemary followed her sister's rules—but with her own interpretation. Once when Martha bought a uniform for Rosemary in grade school that she disliked, for example, Rosemary tried to wear it out to get rid of it, first by tearing it with her hands and, ultimately, by using a razor blade to slice and cut the fabric. When Martha questioned Rosemary about it, Rosemary simply nodded. In truth, she felt more proud of herself than guilty, knowing that she would never have to wear the ugly dress uniform again.

In the grace that comes from God's attention to detail, even the stubbornness and willfulness that has been a part of Rosemary's temperament since her childhood has served her well in adulthood, particularly as she dealt with major issues as the woman in charge of her religious community. Even the internal pep talks that as a little girl kept Rosemary lighthearted and able to shrug off anxiety or worry became ultimately a blessed asset when she needed to respond in obedience to her superiors or face a life-threatening situation. As Sabina repeatedly teased her youngest daughter,

"It's hard for me to know when you're angry, Rosemary, because you laugh even when things are tough!"[3]

According to Sister Rosemary, Martha had also told their parents that she wanted to join a religious order, but Sabina and Martino did not approve. "I understand why they didn't want their first daughter to go," Sister Rosemary recalls. "She was trained as a teacher and at that time my parents didn't have a lot of money to educate all the children. So they said to her, 'Now that you're educated, you have to educate the others.' By the time they got to me," however, she adds laughing, "there was no opposing my religious vocation!"

A Very African Catholic Church

The Catholic faith arrived in northern Uganda thanks to Italian Father Daniel Comboni, whose vocation from an early age called him to become a priest and a missionary to Africa. In 1864, just ten years after becoming a priest, Father Comboni launched a project designed not only to proclaim the Gospel throughout the African continent, but also to prepare Africans to evangelize their own people. "Save Africa with Africa," Father Comboni's motto, was nothing less than a revolutionary idea at that time. Three years later, at age thirty-six, Father Comboni founded the Missionary Institute for men (Sons of the Sacred Heart of Jesus), and in 1872, he founded the Missionary Sisters—the community that Rosemary would one day join. Father Comboni was named the first bishop of central Africa in 1877, with his vicariate based in Khartoum, Sudan, where he died four years later. To put it in historical perspective, Comboni's vision for Africa originated over twenty years before Uganda began its seventy years of British rule as a British protectorate, in 1894.

The Mahdist War prevented Father Comboni from carrying out his project in Uganda, and in 1878, Pope Leo XIII entrusted the area of sub-Saharan Africa to the French cardinal Charles Lavigerie, archbishop of Algiers and Carthage, and to his society, the White Fathers, a name taken from the color of their long tunics. The first institute of women religious was founded in 1878, when Archbishop Lavigerie founded the Missionary Sisters of Our Lady of Africa (or White Sisters) to serve side by side with the White Fathers in Uganda, Tanzania, Zambia, and Algiers—with the White Fathers landing near what is now Entebbe, on Lake Victoria, founding a Catholic mission in 1879. In Uganda, the White Sisters settled at Rubaga in 1899. It wasn't until 1920, more than thirty years after Bishop Comboni's death, that his successor personally guided the first group of Comboni Missionaries among the Alur, coming from Sudan to northern Uganda along the course of the Nile. Often referred to in Uganda as the Verona Fathers, since that's where the head office of their community is located, the Comboni Missionaries opened their northern Uganda mission among the Acholi in Gulu in 1921.

But evangelization and the spread of the Gospel did not come without sacrifice. In 1879, King Mutesa of the Bugandan kingdom (modern-day southern Uganda)—the largest and most powerful of all the tribes—allowed his subjects to choose among all the faiths, including Christianity. In *Butler's Lives of the Saints*, he is described as a "not unfriendly ruler" to the Christian missionaries, and for a time, the missions flourished.

However, after King Mutesa's twenty-four-year reign ended with his death in 1884, his eighteen-year-old son Mwanga became king, a man known for his corruption and for being a practicing pedophile. When the young pages at the palace who had converted to Christianity began to reject his sexual advances, King Mwanga became furious. Over time, he was easily persuaded that Christianity caused the ancestors to be angry at the desertion of the old ways—and he began to eliminate Christianity from the kingdom, persecuting missionaries and the new Christians. A year into his reign, King Mwanga had three Baganda Anglicans dismembered and their bodies burned. Later that same year, the newly arrived Anglican bishop was murdered on Mwanga's orders.

King Mwanga's master of the pages was a Catholic man named Joseph Mukasa, who catechized the younger pages and protected them from the king. He was seized on a pretext and beheaded on November 15, 1885—becoming the first of the black Catholic martyrs on the continent. That same night, twenty-five-year-old Charles Lwanga and some of the other pages went to the White Fathers and asked to be baptized. A few months later, when King Mwanga became aware that the boys were still receiving Christian instruction, he commanded all the pages to appear and then ordered the Christians to be separated. When asked if they intended to remain Christian, fifteen boys and young men between the ages of thirteen and twenty-five said yes, including Charles Lwanga and Kizito, the youngest of the pages. King Mwanga's response was immediate, "Then you shall all burn!"

The boys were bound together and taken to Namugongo, a two-day walk, where they were imprisoned for seven days before being burned at the stake on June 3, 1886, on the feast of the Ascension. King Mwanga continued to torture and murder Christians for several years until he was overthrown by a rebellion. But Mwanga's savagery and the witness of the martyrs ignited an increase in the number of

Christian believers, with an estimated 10,000 Christians in the Buganda kingdom by 1890.[4] In all, twenty-two Catholics and twenty-four Anglican martyrs were killed around that time at Namugongo. Pope Benedict XV recognized the martyrdom of the Catholics and beatified them in 1920. On October 18, 1964, Pope Paul VI canonized all twenty-two of the Catholic martyrs. Five years later he made a pilgrimage to Namugongo, the site of their martyrdom, becoming the first pope to ever visit the African continent.

Two Ugandan martyrs, Daudi Okelo and Jildo Irwa, stand out to Catholics in northern Uganda because these two catechists were members of the Acholi tribe. The teenager Daudi and twelve-year-old Jildo were killed in 1918. After Daudi was killed, Jildo, in tears, said, "We have done nothing wrong. . . . For the same reason you killed Daudi you must also kill me, because together we came here and together we have been teaching God's word." They were beatified by St. Pope John Paul II in 2002 and are still remembered and honored by the local church and missionaries, but in particular by the Combonis whose ministry has been directly with the northern tribes. Father Comboni's was a plan "for the regeneration of Africa by recognizing the dignity and gifts God has given to the people of this continent," explained Father Christian Carlassare, Comboni Missionaries of the Heart of Jesus, vice provincial of South Sudan, at the Mass celebrating the 150th anniversary of Father Comboni's founding of the Institute. "We celebrate this anniversary with gratitude to the Lord for his mercy and compassion for Africa and for his Spirit who lead the Church to finally gain this 'precious black pearl/Africa' as it was called by St Daniel Comboni." Concluding, Father Carlassare added, "And I personally see that the Institute has still a mission ahead at the service of the Universal

Church on the field of first evangelization (in Africa and in the world)."[5]

Uganda's Catholic roots remain, even now, deep in the country's heart. According to a 2011 report on global Christianity by the Pew Research Center, Uganda has 14,100,000 Catholics—that's equivalent to 42.2 percent of the population.[6] The report estimates that around one in five sub-Saharan Africans belonged to the Catholic Church in 2010. And while it is true that the world's Catholic population has grown impressively (by 57 percent) since 1980, according to a 2015 Georgetown University CARA (Center for Applied Research in the Apostolate) report,[7] Africa's Catholic population has more than tripled during that time, approaching 200 million. The report predicts that by 2040, almost one in four Africans will be Catholic, putting the continent's total Catholic population at 460.4 million. In the words of Archbishop John Baptist Odama, head of Uganda's conference of Catholic bishops, "The Church has been a mother [to the African people]. . . . It has been with the people in all their initial stages of life and in their critical conditions."[8]

Leaving Everything Familiar Behind

Rosemary's parents called her back to live with them when she was thirteen years old. In the early 1970s, as teenager Rosemary was discerning what she wanted to do with her life, she made time to pray in the mornings at her parish church, just up the red dirt street from her home. The Paidha parish church of Mary Immaculate has a special place in Sister Rosemary's heart. Her grandparents donated the land where the church was built, and her carpenter father made the doors to the church building. From an early age, Rosemary learned from her family a dedication to daily prayer, to each other as family, and to service through the local parish church. Every night, her family prayed together. And it was her older brothers who taught Rosemary how to pray the rosary, a practice that remains part of her daily routine. Then, as she considered and pondered what it would look like to answer the increasing desire in her heart to do more for God, Rosemary heard about a community of missionary sisters from neighboring Sudan who had a special ministry to the poor and the orphaned, the Comboni Missionary Sisters.

"It's difficult to trace an exact moment because I always say that I do think God calls all of us according to how we are created, or how we listen to his voice," says Sister Rosemary. "The sisters would come to speak to us as young girls, telling us about different congregations and societies and the role of vocation. They used to tell us that if you want to listen to God . . . God can call you to different things, call you to marriage, call you to be a teacher, a doctor, anything—but you have to pray and ask, 'God give me the right call,' and so I did! I heard the right call, and I heard it young!—to the Comboni Sisters.

"I had just turned fifteen when I went! It was very, very early," remembers Sister Rosemary, confessing that "[the sisters] did not know I was that young. The group I entered with was older than me, and I did everything with them," so the sisters simply assumed that Rosemary was older.

Although both her mother and father accepted Rosemary's decision to leave for the convent, it was not the same for her brother Valerio, who had gone to the seminary for a short time before discerning that was not his calling. "He said to me, 'I don't think you have a vocation.' He was so opposed that the evening before I was supposed to leave for the convent, he locked the door with all my things inside the house. When my dad came home from work, I told him that I was supposed to go to Napere to meet the sisters who were taking me to the convent but that I didn't have my things so I couldn't go. My father just said, 'That's not a problem. I have a hammer. I'll break a window! You go in and get your things.' So he did! I went to the convent through a window," she says with a laugh.

Life in Community

Sister Rosemary first came to know of the Italian Comboni Missionary Sisters through her sister Martha, who taught at their school in nearby Napere. "I was scared of them because when I was a child they had given me injections when I was sick," remembers Rosemary with a laugh. "I did not like the white sisters for that!" Yet, she confesses, she was also "attached to them," attached enough and attracted to their charism enough to enter as an aspirant at the age of fifteen. "The Comboni sisters came to Uganda as refugees from Sudan," says Sister Rosemary, adding that the missionaries always planned to go back. Instead, their motherhouse in Juba, South Sudan, has been destroyed twice.

There were many things about Rosemary's new life at the Uganda motherhouse in Moyo that surprised her, and a good number of them that challenged her. In addition to being away from any and all members of her family, Rosemary had never lived in a home without any men. Also, although she looked older than her age, Rosemary was the youngest woman at the convent. "We started as aspirants from one to three years," she explains, "depending on your capability, how you coped with the new life, and how well you understood what was being taught. I was an aspirant for one year," followed by one or two years of postulancy. Rosemary, who was dedicated and driven, was a postulant for one year. The final stage was two years in the novitiate before making their final vows. "They never asked my age, so I made my final vows at nineteen, which I should not have done," says Sister Rosemary, explaining that canon law required that a novice be twenty years old before making final vows. "After I took the vows, Mother said to me, 'Rosemary, we just realized you took the vows before the right age,' but by then they are not reversible," Sister Rosemary adds, grinning.

When Rosemary became an aspirant, the mother superior to the Comboni Missionary sisters was Mother Elizabeth Coggi, who served as superior general from 1963 to 1976. Those were years of learning and growing on many levels and in many areas—especially for a young teenager like Rosemary. "At that time we had few sisters who were educated and prepared to run activities that had been run by the Italian sisters. I had a lot of intuition and was very practical," explains Sister Rosemary. "I learned quickly many things. This mother superior, Elizabeth, she knew that I was very young, but she recognized my potential. I don't know why, but she liked taking me with her! And she liked sending me to do things," often things Rosemary could learn under the Italian Comboni sisters, from learning how to iron to how to bake.

"I knew nothing," Sister Rosemary admits. "I was just a village girl. But I was willing to learn." It was Mother Elizabeth who talked Sister Rosemary into finally cutting her hair, something that was very hard for Rosemary, who had been praised in her younger years for her beautiful tresses. "She talked me into it by saying that I'd be a distraction during prayers—and promising that it would not be too short. It took me a long time to get used to that short hair!" She remembers one time when Mother Elizabeth handed Rosemary her habit and asked her to iron it. "I did my best, but then I said, 'Mother, I'm sorry. I have never ironed a dress for a sister before.' She said to me, 'Rosemary, I take it you did your best—yes? Then I like it.' Her attitude made me want to learn how to really iron so that I'd be ready if she asked me again! They were small, small things— but she took an interest in me!" Rosemary became so good at baking that she was the only girl chosen to travel to an Italian convent to study the art of baking from the nuns.

But Rosemary did not always like her assignments, or even do them. When assigned to take care of the dogs in the convent, Rosemary panicked. Not only did she not have dogs growing up, family lore prohibited anyone in the family from caring for dogs. "I hated the dogs. We were not allowed to have dogs. My mother and father told us that if anyone in our family line was involved in taking care of dogs, it would be a curse, a bad omen—and someone would die."

The fear of dogs began when one of Rosemary's uncles died. His dog loved the man so much that when they took his body away, the dog jumped in to be with him. "That's when my grandfather declared, 'It's a bad omen for a dog to jump on a dead body. From now on, nobody in our family line must care for dogs.' So of course, I go to the convent and it's the first big job they give me!"

In truth, "I considered trying to explain all this to the sisters but decided instead to just not go to the dogs," Sister Rosemary remembers. After several days, Mother Elizabeth found the hungry dogs and she walked straight into the building where the young women were studying, searching for the culprit. "We could hear her yelling from outside, 'Who is in charge of the dogs?'—and the other girls got frightened and turned to me, 'Rosemary, you better go and answer!' So I finally did. Mother looked at me and asked,

"'Rosemary, when did you last eat?'

"I answered, 'I eat every day, Mother.'

"'And when did you last feed the dogs?'

"'But, Mother, I'm afraid of going there!'

"She scolded me in front of everybody. She was tough on me," recalls Sister Rosemary. "But I wasn't going to tell her my real reason! So I went and started to take care of the dogs. I learned." As time passed, Rosemary got in trouble again when assigned to the dogs, but this time it was because she wanted to bake biscuits for them or take towels from the convent for their bedding. "I did, it's true. . . . I started loving the dogs!"

Mother Elizabeth was such an important role model for Rosemary that, in 1989, when Sister Rosemary started a vocational training group to teach the women in Moyo to read and write, she named it Saint Elizabeth Women's Group. What is undeniable is the great impact the Italian Comboni sisters had on Sister's Rosemary's spirit. In addition to demonstrating their dedication to prayer, the sisters modeled for her what it means to be a teacher, a mentor, and a leader: the insistence on excellence; instilling respect for herself and others; an understanding of responsibility; encouraging development of potential—all traits that Sister Rosemary was able to adapt and implement years later in her work with the girls at St. Monica's.

Mother Elizabeth's assistant superior was Sister Annetta Rose Yunith, who went on to become the first African superior general in 1976, the same year that Sister Rosemary took her final vows. "Mother Elizabeth was the last one. I had just become a new sister. I had just taken my vows!" Mother Annetta, the assistant superior, was also the person who led a handful of women as the community transitioned officially, leaving the Comboni congregation to start an African community, the Sacred Heart of Jesus Sisters. They now count over three hundred women in Sudan; Nairobi, Kenya; Uganda; and Phoenix, Arizona, the first community in the United States. "Mother Annetta was so, so good," Sister Rosemary recalls. "She was so prayerful! She also had poor health for a long time. She was delicate." Mother Annetta died in 1979. She was followed by Mother Theresina Ihure, who served as second superior general until 1994.

Sister Doreen Oyella, who entered the convent at the much older age of eighteen, has known Sister Rosemary since those early years in the convent, before either of them had become sisters—although Sister Rosemary is quick to point out that although they are the same age, Sister Rosemary is "much ahead of [Sister Doreen] in religious vocation. I entered earlier." After a lifetime of "growing up together" and forty-one years as Sacred Heart Sisters, the two women have endless stories of their work, and they laugh often telling those stories. After all these decades in the convent, notes Sister Doreen, "We must have done something right. Nothing comes from nothing," she says with a smile, quoting a song from the musical *The Sound of Music,* a favorite of both of women.

Looking back at those first few years in community, when they were both so young, the women say the difficulties they faced were very real, even if a bit childlike. For Doreen, it was the calm atmosphere and the order of it all. "I'm very lively, and I like running! I had a hard time when I first joined. You are supposed to walk s-l-o-w-l-y, gently, learn humility that way. I was very stubborn!"

But for Rosemary it was more about her candor. As the priest who led spiritual formation told her, "Rosemary, you are very frank, and you are as you are. You will be in trouble many times!"

Ultimately, the tales of those years tell a story of two young women who did not know how much they didn't know until they went to the convent in Moyo. Yet it was their heart that each of them followed. Today, they are in awe at the place where God has brought them, and at the fact they are still together! As Sister Rosemary notes, "Friendship is such an important thing." Observation makes it abundantly clear how important humor is for both women, especially in light of the many critical and major events that they have faced together.

"I'm going to use some of the money from my latest speech for a storehouse/room," Sister Rosemary says to her old friend, Sister Doreen.

"Thank you for your generosity," Sister Doreen jokes with a straight smile, as she passes her friend a plate of sliced papaya. And they both laugh. "Divine Providence, Sister. Holy Providence of God, help us," Sister Doreen adds.

"That doesn't make sense," Rosemary immediately quips back. "I don't see how Holy Providence can help you. If it's God the Father who is provident, who is going to help you? Father Most Provident, help us. That is faith. . . . That's why we say, 'Holy Providence of God help us' fifty time every day."

"I do it thirty," Doreen retorts back, confessing.

"That's a shortcut!" Rosemary exclaims, then laughs and laughs.

One is a "woman of night" and the other a "woman of morning," making it hard for the two friends to do something as simple as watch a movie together when they are both in Gulu. But they both agree on the importance of their communal, common prayer—something the Sacred Heart

Sisters do together daily whether there are two or ten sisters available for morning and evening prayer.

"There are people who get up early and start reading. I can't do that. I have to read in the evening and sleep with it," explains Sister Rosemary. "Another thing that puts me to bed is the rosary. Have you ever finished a rosary in your bed?" she says, turning to look at her friend of forty-four years. "I start many rosaries," says Sister Rosemary with a laugh. "My rosary goes everywhere with me. A good place to sit and pray is under the mango tree."

"That *is* a good place," Sister Doreen nods, suddenly turning serious. "Rosemary," she pauses, "you have a motherly heart."

Outside the Convent's Walls, Trouble Brews

Uganda became an independent country in 1962, with Apollo Milton Obote as prime minister and Buganda's King Mutesa as president. In 1966, Obote seized power in a coup, ending the autonomy of the Buganda kingdom, abolishing other Ugandan tribal kingdoms—and promoting himself to the presidency. But in 1971, the same year that Sister Rosemary entered the convent, Ugandan armed forces commander Idi Amin Dada Oumee overthrew the government of Obote in a military coup and shortly thereafter declared himself president of Uganda, for life.

Amin, a member of the Kakwa tribe who was also a Muslim, was a violent ruler and an egomaniac who recruited many followers from his own ethnic group. When Britain broke diplomatic relations with Uganda, for example, Amin declared that he had defeated the British and added "CBE" (Conqueror of the British Empire) to his title—making his entire title "His Excellency President for Life, Field Marshal Alhaji Dr. Idi Amin Dada, VC, DSO, MC, CBE."

Amin's wrath fell upon vast numbers—ethnic groups, religious leaders, journalists, artists, intellectuals, foreign nationals, and others. He also ordered mass executions of Acholi and Lango ethnic people, as well as Christian tribes that had been traditionally loyal to Obote. By early 1972, approximately 5,000 Acholi and Lango soldiers, and at least twice as many civilians, had disappeared. That same year, Amin issued a decree ordering the expulsion of 60,000 Asians who were not Ugandan citizens. The spree of killings that Amin pursued were broadly motivated by ethnic, political, and financial factors. Although the exact number of people killed throughout his eight years in control is unknown, the International Commission of Jurists estimated the death toll at no fewer than 80,000 and more likely around 300,000. An estimate compiled by Amnesty International, however, estimates the number to be as high as 500,000.[9]

From 1971 until 1979, when Amin was finally ousted from power by Tanzanian troops, Amin's reign of violence and viciousness permeated Uganda. People would simply disappear, their bodies dumped savagely into the Nile River. US Ambassador Thomas Patrick Melady recommended as early as 1973 that the United States reduce its presence in Uganda. After he described Amin's regime as "racist, erratic and unpredictable, brutal, inept, bellicose, irrational, ridiculous, and militaristic," the US finally closed its embassy in Kampala.[10]

During these years, and almost exactly in a parallel timeline, Rosemary Nyirumbe was an aspirant, postulant, novice, and a newly vowed still-in-training Sacred Heart of Jesus Sister, keeping her somewhat sheltered from the horrors taking place—or at least, keeping her from being directly impacted. But in the late 1970s everything was about to change.

CHAPTER TWO

A Comboni Spirituality
(1976–1986)

For his Apostles, the winds shook and the room
filled as tongues came to rest on them. He moves
my heart and, just as with them, his spirit rests on
me. He speaks his love language in ways my heart
will not miss, and assures me he will not pass by
unnoticed—the winds will shake and the room will
be filled.

Jennifer Hubbard, "Pentecost Sunday," *Magnificat*

Landlocked Uganda encompasses an area roughly
150,000 square miles, slightly larger than the state of Mon-
tana. But if you take away its vast lakes and other water
mass, the entire land area of the country is actually just a
little bigger than New Mexico. Located on the northern
edge of the equator in East Africa, Uganda is bordered on
the east by Kenya, on the north by South Sudan, on the west
by the Democratic Republic of the Congo, on the southwest
by Rwanda, and on the south by Tanzania. The southern
part of the country includes a substantial portion of Lake

Victoria, which is also bordered by Kenya and Tanzania. In 1894, British officials adopted the name Uganda, the Swahili term for Buganda—which is the largest ethnic group in the country—when they established the Uganda Protectorate. The region had previously been placed under the charter of the Imperial British East Africa Company by the United Kingdom. But Uganda was never conquered in the colonial era. Instead, it was the powerful king (or kabaka) Mutesa who made a deal with the British that gave the Buganda kingdom protectorate status. Under British colonial rule, it became the unofficial policy to use Buganda chiefs to oversee their business.[1] This means that Luganda remains the most common language, and English is the country's official language.

The history of Catholicism in Uganda was also directly affected by British colonial rule. Although the Catholic White Fathers missionaries arrived in the region in 1879, Imperial British East Africa Company agent Frederick Lugard extended the company's control to southern Uganda and helped the Protestant missionaries to prevail over the Catholic communities. Six years after Uganda became a British protectorate, in 1900, Britain signed an agreement with the Buganda kingdom giving it autonomy and turning it into a constitutional monarchy controlled mainly by Protestant chiefs.[2]

Although several territories and tribes were integrated in 1914 to form the basis of what we now know as Uganda, the country remains a quilt of cultural diversity. There are (officially) seventeen tribes recognized in modern-day Uganda, and they can be classified into two broad groups: the Bantu speaking tribes, including the large Baganda tribe, and the Nilotic language kingdoms—which include the Acholi, Langi, Lugbara, Madi, Kakwa, and the Alur, the tribe that Sister Rosemary and her family belong to. The Nilotic speaking people entered the region from the north, probably beginning about AD 100. They were the first cattle-herding people in the area, although they have also always relied on crop cultivation to supplement their subsistence. As Sister Rosemary points out, northern Uganda is very poor—but the people are not hungry. There are two wet seasons, providing plenty of rainfall, and the soil quality is good enough that crops are grown for consumption and for export. There is no food storage available, however, since most people do not have electricity or refrigerators, and a lot of fresh food is thrown away. The Alur, who live west of the Acholi and the Langi, are culturally similar to neighboring societies of the West Nile region.[3] The British may have created artificial borders to make distinct countries, but Uganda tribes and their kingdoms cross national borders.

What tribe a person comes from is the first and biggest personal identifier in Ugandan culture, with language being a close second. For Sister Rosemary this means that her intellectual ability and knowledge of more than six languages or dialects have served her well in her very different assignments. All Sacred Heart of Jesus Sisters are supposed to know, or learn, Swahili as well as other languages, depending on their location and their work. English is the community's common language, but Arabic is the second language of their congregation, because of their work in South Sudan.

In 1977, the year after Sister Rosemary made her vows as a sister, she and two other sisters, Seraphine and Pierina, were sent to gain medical experience at the Angal Hospital in the West Nile. She was twenty-one years old. On her first day at the medical facility, Sister Rosemary was assigned to the maternity ward, a place and a service that she immediately fell in love with. She was so good at it, in fact, that after that one year of training was over, she was assigned to the Kalongo School of Nursing and Midwifery in the Gulu district to become certified as a midwife. Founded in 1944 by the Comboni Missionary sisters as a small dispensary, St. Mary's Midwifery Training School, as the facility is called today, was the region's first organized health care. From its beginnings in a grass hut, it evolved over the years into separate maternity and medical units. In 1959, an Italian Comboni priest who was also a medical doctor, Dr. Giuseppe Ambrosoli, expanded it to the midwifery school it is today as a way to address the area's high mortality rates in maternity and childbirth. Following Bishop Comboni's ideal, "Save Africa with Africa," the school has graduated 1,167 midwifes and is considered the finest training facility in Uganda.[4]

Sister Rosemary not only learned how to deliver babies, she adored doing it! And she loved helping women give birth. But most of all, she loved spending time in the nursery with the newborns. Her sharp eyes and steady hand also caught the attention of Dr. Ambrosoli, who unofficially trained her as his assistant in the operating theater—teaching her skills that would come to serve her well not far into her future. "She was brave and very capable in the operating theatre," remembers Sister Rumilde, an eighty-nine-year-old Italian with over sixty-five years as a Comboni Missionary, who was a nurse when Sister Rosemary was at the hospital. Sister Rumilde, now retired and living in Gulu, has not been surprised by everything that Sister Rosemary has been able to accomplish. Like many of the other missionaries, Sister Rumilde may be a "Mzungu" (pronounced "muh-zun-goo"), the Uganda word for a white person, but she refuses to go back to Italy. She emphasizes that Uganda is her life—and she plans to die there.

"I Go Where God Wants Me to Go"

In late October 1978, Uganda president Idi Amin ordered an attack on Tanzania, seeking to expand his kingdom. But Tanzanian government troops, assisted by Ugandan exiles, crushed the Ugandan army—continuing their routing and defeat all the way to Kampala, Uganda's capital. In April 1979, Amin's government was overthrown by Tanzanian soldiers and he fled the city, escaping first to Libya before finally seeking sanctuary in Saudi Arabia. The years following Amin's reign of terror consisted of several short-term Ugandan presidencies and overthrows, almost always dictated by tribe and government faction. It was a long, unstable period of guerrilla warfare. Even for those living in northern Uganda, explains Sister Rosemary, the waves of power moving through the capital in south Uganda were simply too temporary to be noted two hundred miles away.

"Sometimes it was difficult to even follow" who was in charge of the country, she explained. "You'd hear someone was in the government; then two weeks later they were gone!" At the same time during these volatile years, an ill-paid, ill-disciplined, and vengeful army consisting largely of Acholi and Lango soldiers who had been persecuted by Amin ravaged the Ugandan countryside looting and taking vengeance on their longtime enemies, while remnants of Amin's supporters formed rebel groups in the West Nile region. Across the land, civilians were the ones caught in the middle. In December 1980, Milton Obote once again rose into a second presidency, but the instability and questionable government power continued.

When in 1981 Sister Rosemary completed her medical training and was assigned to her first official ministry at a medical clinic in Moyo, she found that the ongoing guerrilla warfare in the region had left the West Nile town nearly deserted. The town she went to was a very different Moyo than the one she encountered as a fifteen-year-old aspirant entering the convent. "The Moyo I knew was a peaceful Moyo. I became a nun and went to do my training as a midwife and came back, but that, that was a very difficult Moyo," Sister Rosemary remembers. With the border only twenty miles away, many Moyo residents had fled north to safety in what is now South Sudan. Even their community members had left for their motherhouse in Juba. "Most of our sisters ran to Sudan as refugees, but because Sister Veronica and I had been away in training, very far away, the two of us had remained in Uganda at the school."

According to United Nations figures, in 1983 there were 260,000 refugees from West Nile in what was then one country called Sudan and in Zaire, now known as the Democratic Republic of the Congo, but the true figure was probably much higher. One of the most documented incidents of violence in West Nile occurred at the Ombaci Catholic mission, near Arua, in June 1981. According to a 1989 Amnesty International report on Uganda, "Several thousand displaced people had already taken refuge at the mission when a group of anti-government guerrillas came there for medical treatment. Representatives of the International Committee of the Red Cross agreed to their request on humanitarian grounds. Shortly after the guerrillas left the mission, a group of UNLA [Uganda National Liberation Army] soldiers attacked it, killing sixty unarmed civilians (half of them children) in the compound, church, and school." The massacre attracted international attention because of the presence of Red Cross delegates at the mission. During the next four years, reports reaching Amnesty International from the West Nile region suggested that "the incident had been by no means atypical."[5]

For the general population, it was a complicated military situation, not easy to understand. As Sister Rosemary explains, it was often hard to differentiate insurgents from real military. The Comboni sisters, who had founded the residence decades earlier, were no longer in charge of the Moyo mission. They had turned over the reins to their offspring, the Sacred Heart of Jesus Sisters—and within a year, most everyone had left, leaving Sister Rosemary to run the dispensary by herself. There was one doctor, she adds, but he was a drunk and therefore unreliable, requiring her to make all urgent medical decisions. Yet being able to speak the local Madi as well as the Lwo languages gave her a unique ability to communicate with both patients and soldiers, who were often one and the same. With the nearest hospital many miles away, at the dispensary Sister Rosemary became medically a jack-of-all-trades.

"We had a lot of rebels coming down from Sudan and fighting against the army soldiers. It was all tribal. In Moyo they are Madi, and most government soldiers were Acholi," remembers Sister Rosemary. "For me, it was a very difficult situation. I was trying to work with the soldiers. I would go to the barracks with the priests to pray, to translate their preaching. They needed someone who could communicate with all of them with no fear, and that was me!"

The people in Moyo were afraid of the soldiers, and the soldiers could not speak the language of the people. "It was the same type of violence as the rebels, but these were soldiers. The Uganda National Liberation Army, comprised of a lot of Acholi soldiers, were revenging what Idi Amin had done to them, so while they were serving in the government in West Nile, they were taking a lot of revenge, stealing people's property, setting houses on fire, causing a lot of atrocities and killing people." Sister Rosemary's natural smile is absent as she recalls, "It was terrible. I had to work hard to try even to speak with the rebels, begging them not to harm people. Things were so bad . . . I got caught up in that stressful situation there. Yet there was nothing I could do." In the middle of all the violence, trying to take care of the needs of people on both sides, Sister Rosemary also felt responsible for the safety of her sisters and the children in their care.

Sister Rosemary will never forget one instance when government solders passing by broke into their property in the evening. "We saw them through the windows and we ran and hid ourselves in our bedrooms." The two men walked to the dispensary and began bagging some of the medicine from the infirmary. They walked to the orphanage and collected as many things, including mattresses, as they could carry. "I saw them and I knew them. But I said to the sisters, 'They are uniformed men with guns. Let's let them do what they're going to do and not go out and get ourselves in trouble,'" she remembers. But the next day, Sister Rosemary went to talk to the commanding officer. She told him, "Sir, two of your men stole things from the orphanage and the dispensary last night; even the milk of the children was taken. It was too much."

"How do you know they were soldiers?" he questioned her.

"I saw uniformed men. They were not rebels. They are not thieves. They were soldiers."

The commanding officer went to the barracks and gave an order to look for everything that had been stolen. They found many of the things that Sister Rosemary had mentioned and then returned to Sister Rosemary.

"Sister, we found your thieves," he admitted. That afternoon soldiers brought back two pickup trucks full of stolen things, setting them under the mango tree by the entrance. "They asked me to come and identify the thieves and I said, 'I don't want to come, because if I do, I'm going to slap each one of them!' But the commanding officer asked me, 'What do you want us to do with them?' I said, 'You can do whatever you want. I just want the things that were stolen.' What's funny is that they did bring back everything—including things that had been stolen two years before!"

A Spiritual Friendship for All Time

In 1983, thirty-seven-year-old Comboni Father Luigi Gabaglio was sent to Uganda from his native Italy and was assigned to Moyo, where he met a spunky Ugandan sister ten years younger than him who was proficiently and efficiently in charge. The two of them have been making history together ever since. "I quickly learned that whatever needed to be done, she was the one to ask," says Father Luigi with a smile. "At one point everybody in town knew me by name," Sister Rosemary explains. "I was running the dispensary, running the clinic. There was no hospital; it was abandoned when everyone ran away. There was no doctor. People were lying everywhere around our clinic." Because there was no doctor, both rebels and soldiers turned to her for help. "I had no fear of really telling them off or speaking with them," stresses Sister Rosemary. "For one thing, I had them in my hand. They came to me at the dispensary. I had to deliver their wives in the barracks. All of that gave me authority over them too."

Not long after Sister Rosemary met Father Luigi, a woman carrying two bleeding young men stumbled into the dispensary. The woman was their mother, and she told Sister Rosemary that someone had thrown a hand grenade at them. "I told the mother, 'I will do the best that I can.' But

I needed all kinds of help, so I called for other sisters and for father to come help me. I gave Father Luigi a lamp to hold. . . . It really was a horrible situation. The boys were screaming terribly, there was blood everywhere, and I was removing splinters from their skin. That's when I looked over and saw Father Luigi fainting!"

Or as he likes to describe it now, remembering that intense moment, "The lamp was swaying!" says Father Luigi, who just smiles at his friend Rosemary, as he shrugs his shoulders. "I could not bear blood!" Needless to say, Sister Rosemary continues, "I sent him out and called for someone else to hold the lamp!"

In addition to running the medical clinic and dispensary, Sister Rosemary took on the task of helping update the orphanage, an adjacent building originally built in 1947 by the Comboni Missionary sisters—making it the oldest orphanage in Uganda. While the structure needed repair, the biggest challenge they faced was the large number of children. Some had been orphaned by either rebel or government soldiers. Others had been left behind by their parents as they fled the fighting, and then crossed north to what was then Sudan. Still others, some of the youngest babies there, had been left by parents who felt burdened, incapable of feeding one more child.

The Moyo Babies Home took them all in, including babies as young as a few days old. At the orphanages, Sister Rosemary explains, "We take kids who were abandoned—take them from zero to five, hoping one day a relative will come up or someone may want to adopt kids and take care of them. But that really rarely happens." For children with special needs, "We offer them temporary care until we can find them a home. We take all children who are abandoned." When they reach school age, "We transfer them to a children's home where we care for them like one of our own children, educate them, and help them become useful members of the society. Once they finish their education, they can go on and settle in society."

Sister Rosemary ran the Moyo dispensary and clinic for three years and then was transferred to the community's medical clinic in Adjumani, a small town approximately twenty miles south of Moyo, across the Nile River. Without a bridge, a ferry connects the two communities. "I didn't stay in Moyo very long, but for me that time in Moyo was so hectic! I dealt with so many things . . . all at the same time. I slept in the front," says Sister Rosemary softly, as if recalling a dream, "close to the door, so that I could run out as needed. I used to look from the house in the night and come to treat patients. It was very unsafe. We had no electricity. I would come and deliver women just with a flashlight." She pauses before adding, "It was all very, very difficult."

Father Luigi and Sister Rosemary have been close friends ever since their stint together during those tumultuous years in Moyo. She also considers him her mentor. "He has been a great support to me in many, many ways," says Sister Rosemary, noting that she was still in her twenties when they met and faced all those difficulties in Moyo. "It was a hard time. And really, I had a lot of responsibilities. The sisters that were with me, it was a challenge for them as well. But I was the superior at the home. I suffered but made it through it. And he, Father Luigi, was a good support for me . . . every time." Some of the difficulties, ironically, were with other Comboni Missionaries, who dismissed her because of her age—or because she was a woman. "I remember once they wanted to make a decision and asked me to leave. It was a strange moment." But Father Luigi, who was the priest assigned and in charge, said "No! She stays." During those difficult times, "when some of the [other], older, Comboni missionary priests would not understand me, Father Luigi was like a bridge!"

Developing a Comboni Spirituality

For Father Luigi, Sister Rosemary's unique understanding of the Comboni Missionary spirit is not solely based on her lengthy, lifetime relationship with the missionaries, both men and women. When Father Luigi was assigned to the border town of Moyo, he was there to replace a popular priest, Father Osmundo Bilbao Nierajo, who had been killed in an ambush traveling to Kampala. In addition to taking care of the parish, the inexperienced Father Luigi was asked to help the sisters in their mission at the medical clinic and the orphanage. Sister Rosemary welcomed him with open arms. And that, Father Luigi notes, is how Sister Rosemary encounters everything she faces in life, "with open arms. That's Comboni!"

"We've been following each other since Moyo," Father Luigi notes matter-of-factly, trying to find words to describe the deep respect and affection that he and Sister Rosemary have for one another. "We have developed a deep trust in each other. She challenges me, yes!" Perhaps the thing about Sister Rosemary that stands out the most for Father Luigi is what he calls her "Comboni spirituality," noting Sister Rosemary's balance of service and prayer. From the time he first arrived in Moyo in 1983 as a young priest to work with Father Luigi Benedetti at the mission parish, Father Luigi says he recognized something unique in the small nun who took charge of things. It wasn't so much about all the things that she did, but more about *how* she did them, even as a young sister.

The Sisters of the Sacred Heart of Jesus, whose "inspiration is Comboni," have been richly shaped by his nun friend from Paidha, Father Luigi points out about Sister Rosemary. "She has a special communication with the poor, something which she does in a unique way that others cannot. She has a total dedication to the people, to the poorest ones among us. She gives herself completely to the work of the sisters, wherever she has been assigned. And she exemplifies what Father Comboni tried to express when he said, 'Save Africa with Africa.'" Father Luigi also admires Sister Rosemary's ability to learn new tasks, including so many languages. Although he has spent his entire priestly life in Uganda, Father Luigi has never been able to master Madi or any of the other dialects spoken in the country's northern region, in what he stresses is, ironically, his true home.

Reflecting on what it means to have a Comboni spirit, Father Luigi points to how Bishop Comboni fell in love with Africa. The fact that an Italian from Limone sul Garda, Italy, could become entranced with the mission to central Africa before he had ever been there, notes Father Luigi, is itself a sign that his inspiration came from the Holy Spirit.

It wasn't until three years after being ordained that Father Comboni undertook a four-month journey to Khartoum, capital of Sudan. "The impact of this first face-to-face encounter with Africa is tremendous," notes the official Vatican biography on St. Daniel Comboni. Father Comboni is immediately made aware of the multiple difficulties that are part of his new mission. "But labours, unbearable climate, sickness, the deaths of several of his young fellow-missionaries, the poverty and dereliction of the population, only serve to drive him forward, never dreaming of giving up what he has taken on with such great enthusiasm. From the mission of Holy Cross he wrote to his parents: 'We will have to labour hard, to sweat, to die: but the thought that one sweats and dies for love of Jesus Christ and the salvation of the most abandoned souls in the world, is far too sweet for us to desist from this great enterprise.'"[6]

* * *

Sister Rosemary worked at the clinic in Adjumani for only one year before she asked for permission to go back to school to finish her secondary studies, with the hopes of one day putting all her medical knowledge to work by becoming a certified paramedic. The community agreed, and she was assigned to Sacred Heart Secondary School in Gulu, a place where she could do ministry while also taking the courses she needed.

CHAPTER THREE

Little Things with Great Love
(1987–2000)

> This is why I want you, as I said, to be engulfed and
> set on fire in him, constantly gazing into the gentle
> eye of his charity. . . . Lift up, lift up your puny
> heart, your small disordered conscience! Don't give
> any leverage to the wicked devil, who wants to pre-
> vent so much good and doesn't want to be thrown
> out of this city. No, I want you, with courageous
> heart and perfect zeal, to realize that the Holy Spir-
> it's law is quite different from ours.
>
> St. Catherine of Siena, in Suzanne Noffke, OP,
> *The Letters of Catherine of Siena*

Located in northwestern Uganda, Gulu is the marketing
center for the main agricultural region in the north and the
largest town in northern Uganda. While newly paved roads
now connect it to Kampala, Uganda's capital city 208 miles
to its south, when Sister Rosemary arrived in Gulu at the
end of 1986, the crumbling roads made it an eight-hour
journey. Gulu is the heartland of the Acholi tribe, and it is

often referred to as Acholiland. Approximately 70 percent of the population in this region is Catholic. Historically, under British rule, northern Uganda was viewed as a marginal and primitive region. Whereas the Baganda people in the south were favored as colonial administrators, the British often employed Acholi as manual unskilled labor or recruited them into the uniformed services to serve in the army, police, and as prison guards—which, ironically, made other tribes resent them. Acholi soldiers were even part of the British military in World War II. Following Ugandan independence, the region continued to be marginalized economically, suffering higher rates of poverty than other parts of the country. Approximately 90 percent of the people who live in the Gulu district reside in rural areas.

The year before Sister Rosemary went to Gulu, President Milton Obote was deposed in a military coup. He was replaced by Tito Okello, whose presidency was exceptionally brief. A mere few months later, the National Resistance Army (NRA) rebels invaded Uganda's capital city and took over Kampala, installing Yoweri Museveni as president of Uganda on January 29, 1986—and marking the beginning of a long period of relative political stability that continues to this day. Museveni's father belonged to the Banyankole tribe and his mother to the Banyarwanda tribe, both subgroups of the Bantu peoples. He was born in a village in the Ankole province, in southwest Uganda, and most of his NRA soldiers were peasants from the south and the west. At his inauguration, President Museveni promised a new government, a "fundamental change in the politics" of the country, not another mere "change of the guard."[1]

In the meantime, a major instability was rapidly brewing in northern Uganda—a rebel war even more violent and deadly than all others before it. Acholi priestess and rebel leader Alice (Auma) Lakwena, founder of the cultlike Holy Spirit Movement or Holy Spirit Mobile Forces, was a self-proclaimed mystic who claimed to be channeling a powerful warrior spirit that could make her soldiers invulnerable. She took on the name "Lakwena," Acholi for "messenger," and in 1986 launched a rebellion against President Museveni. The daughter of a Madi father and an Acholi mother, Lakwena was only twenty-eight years old when she founded the Holy Spirit Movement and its resistance crusade. Her philosophy included the belief that the Acholi never surrender—and that the Acholi tribe was meant to overthrow the government and retake power in Kampala. She told her soldiers that, according to her messages from God, the Acholi needed purification—exhorting a "pure, clean Acholi youth" that would redeem the Acholi people. Alice Lakwena's "Holy Spirit Safety precautions" for her soldiers included rubbing their chests with shea butter oil to shield themselves against bullets; transforming stones into exploding grenades by placing them in pails of water; singing Christian hymns as they marched into battle; and killing no bees or snakes, considered allies of the Holy Spirit Movement.[2]

When President Museveni's soldiers defeated her troops in 1987, Lakwena fled to Kenya, where she was first detained and later granted political asylum. But many of her followers simply switched to join the rebel forces of Acholi militant Joseph Kony, whose movement would one day become the infamous and horrific Lord's Resistance Army (LRA).

In the Name of God

Sister Rosemary went to Gulu in 1986 seeking an opportunity to attend school. She requested permission from her community to finish the secondary education she had left when she entered the convent at age fifteen, thereby completing her formal education. Sacred Heart Secondary School was founded by Comboni sisters in 1934 as a primary school for girls, the first in northern Uganda. The school was a pioneer, offering education "at a time when no opportunities were being given to girls," noted Sister Mary Carla Ajio, who became a head teacher at the school in 1982. In an article published in November 2001, Ajio acknowledged that "the standard of the school dropped from 1986 to around 1993," as boarding students and faculty lived in fear of being abducted by Joseph Kony's army as it grew in power in the region. "Many students transferred to other schools in safe areas. It was the first time students were being abducted from the school environment in Gulu."[3]

Sister Rosemary's first brush with the violent political storms exploding throughout northern Uganda began the moment she left Moyo for her new assignment in Gulu. Father Luigi had arranged for a group of volunteers from a British non-governmental organization (NGO) to give Sister Rosemary a ride from Moyo to her new home at Sacred Heart Secondary School. But on their way back from Gulu, after dropping off Sister Rosemary, the NGO vehicle was ambushed by rebel forces and the volunteers were abducted and taken to Sudan—and from there, no one knows what happened to them. They simply disappeared, recalls Sister Rosemary.

It is impossible to overstate the horrors and casualties caused by Joseph Kony and his rebels. Although the year and location are debated, it is believed that Kony was born in 1961 in the village of Odek, about thirty miles from Gulu, and that he is a relative—probably a cousin—of the anti-government militant Alice Lakwena.

By 1988, twenty-six-year-old Kony and his followers had already become a formidable rebel movement, the start of what became the longest and most destructive of Uganda's northern wars. Kony preached a message similar to Lakwena's, insisting that he received messages from God and proclaiming that his army was fighting in the name of God to overthrow the government in order to create a new constitution based on the Ten Commandments. Kony claims to be a spirit medium who is guided by a sort of "spirit general staff," a band of spirits that includes a Sudanese female, a Chinese deputy chief, and two American spirits. Kony's mother was Anglican, and his father had been a Catholic catechist. He had a brother who was a witch doctor, and Kony is said to believe that he inherited his brother's powers after his brother's death.[4] The strategy of Kony and his army was to use terror to stop all form of normal cultural functions, rendering Uganda ungovernable—and keeping more than 15 percent of the country in constant turmoil. The one thing that is clear is that they specialized in the slaughter of innocent people.

In spite of the periodic religious rhetoric uttered by Kony, his movement was best described as a cult, where members were forced to obey and were rewarded only after they proved their loyalty to him and to his orders. If Kony's movement had an ideology, it is impossible to define, let alone understand. For example, although Kony is himself an Acholi, and he claimed to want to form a government led by the Acholi and based on the Ten Commandments, his soldiers attacked and ransacked homes, schools, and businesses across northern Uganda, where Acholi are the predominant tribe.

Kony taught disdain for all education, seeing it as unneeded and unwanted of anyone who is his true follower.

In Gulu alone, the LRA's path of destruction included destroying over one hundred primary schools and killing over one hundred teachers in the district. Since its rise to power in the late 1980s, the LRA committed widespread human rights violations, including murder, abduction, mutilation, and child sex slavery. Kony and his military's violent acts took much from their fellow Acholi—everything from family members and homes to freedom and food or any sense of normalcy. They looted and burned to the ground any village they entered, often setting homes ablaze with the inhabitants locked inside; once they shot at and stopped a bus on the way to Kampala, pulling out passengers to hack them to death. The horror stories are endless.

Little by little, northern Uganda, and in particular the Gulu district where Sister Rosemary lived, had evolved into a lawless region where stealing, plundering, kidnapping, and killing became not only recurrent events, but incidents to be anticipated, even expected. Stories of rebel soldiers entering a village to take people and food into the bush were now commonplace—interrupted only by glorified stories of attacks and battles between government forces and the insurgents. During this period in the late 1980s, Joseph Kony's movement emerged as the Lord's Salvation Army, but taking on several other names over the years, including Uganda People's Christian Democratic Army, or Uganda Democratic Christian Army (UDCA). Finally in 1991, Kony's guerillas became the Lord's Resistance Army, by which it is known today. Whatever name they went by, Kony and his followers had solidified into a scary and malevolent militia.

At Sacred Heart school, Sister Rosemary and three other sisters shared a residence located just a few meters from the school, but very near the walking path and main road. In one long building, the sisters' community quarters housed a chapel, small rooms for meetings, a living room and a dining room, and small private bedrooms at the end of the hallway. The kitchen was in a separate building, next to a small vegetable garden, with banana and mango trees hovering for shade. In addition to attending daytime classes, Sister Rosemary was in charge of maintaining the house, overseeing the sisters, and providing the girls with spiritual guidance when needed.

Because of the school's location, it was not unusual for rebel soldiers to create a walking path through the grounds. This meant ample opportunities for them to create havoc, often storming into a classroom and sending the girls into hiding or even walking into the chapel to disrupt their liturgies. Some days the sisters did not feel safe even leaving their building, so they would read and cook inside the double-walled corridor inside their home, hoping this would make it more difficult for stray bullets to enter. As early as 5 p.m. in the evening, the women would gather, often sleeping at night on the floor huddled together, all in their quest for a deeper feeling of safety.

Without them even noticing, fear and dread had become a new normal for the sisters in a world sabotaged by uncertainty and violence. Once, as the rebels opened the door to the bathroom where all four women were hiding, the sisters screamed so loud that the startled men just ran away. Not only could they hear the bombs exploding near and far away, the women could hear voices through the walls of their building as the soldiers talked while walking down the street. The rebels regularly broke into their house looking for money, medicine, and even mattresses. Most days it was just too dangerous to leave the compound. To make matters worse, it was impossible to distinguish rebels from Uganda government soldiers, since the LRA militia could be wearing uniforms stolen from the army.

Another double-edged sword was the fact that some of the soldiers knew Sister Rosemary by name. "Those government soldiers I treated at the clinic in Moyo," delivering their wives' babies and translating for them in the barracks, had now defected—and had become LRA rebels. "It was three years of really mental torture and fear," Sister Rosemary recalls somberly of her time at Sacred Heart School. "I lived every day, always fighting."

The Root of Courage Is Heart

In 1987, aware that the dangerous "new normal" was affecting their inner peace and numbing their spirits, Sister Rosemary told the sisters it was time to do something productive, "something useful that would always remain," and something that would distract them from the constant fear and get their minds on anything else. Creating a mix of masonry cement and water, the four women built a low brick wall that could serve as a buffer against flooding in the rainy season. "I kept thinking of the movie I saw, *The Bridge on the River Kwai*,[5] where the bridge was built by prisoners," explains Sister Rosemary. "We were not engineers! But we built a compound and made bricks, during a war, with no money. We were suffering, waiting for rebels to come, for gunshots to come. It was important that we do something with nothing—and it is something that remains even today!"

That same year, LRA rebels abducted seven Sacred Heart Secondary School girls. Although the students were released after one week, the community's sense of safety and protection had been completely shattered. Even walking into town for supplies became a major battle. Once, as the sisters walked back to the school carrying their purchases, Sister Rosemary recognized one of the soldiers heading their way. They were rebels returning from an attack in a nearby village, and he was a former officer of the Ugandan army. Sister Rosemary was close enough to hear him say, "That is Rosemary."

One of the men replied, "How do you know her?"

"She is our doctor," said the man, who was now an LRA commander. Then he turned to Sister Rosemary and asked, "Are you here in Gulu now?"

"Yes, I am," Sister Rosemary replied, smiling without stopping to talk. The rebels did nothing to stop her and the sisters.

But later that evening the man came to their building and asked for her. "Sister, the next time we are going to attack, I will let you know. Stay in the house and do not go outside. You all will be safe." He was true to his word, warning Sister Rosemary two different times about guerrilla assaults.[6] Sister Rosemary and Sister Lily Grace, who was also from the Alur tribe, could communicate with most of the rebels. But Sister Alice, a Madi native, and Sister Devota, a Lugbara native, had an added element to their anxiety because they could not understand or speak Acholi, the rebels' language.

One of the most serious attacks took place one afternoon as rebels and Ugandan government soldiers exchanged heavy gunfire in town. Running to get away from the fighting and the stray bullets, people stormed the sisters' building looking for safety. The sisters hid them in the chapel, in the meeting rooms, in the sisters' private rooms—anywhere there was room. After three hours, and with only the sounds of silence in the streets, Sister Rosemary decided it was time to step outside to discern the situation.

"I'm going to open the door and see if anything is happening or if I can see any people," she told the sisters.

"No, don't go! What if they're waiting for you?"

She knew the sisters might be right. But she also knew that the people they were hiding were getting hungry and they were deadly afraid. "I'll be fine. We can't remain like this," she said, stepping out toward the next building, where the kitchen was located. The door to the kitchen was ajar, and Sister Rosemary knew it had been closed when the gunfire began.

She pushed the door open and stepped into the kitchen just as a rebel soldier was coming out. Taking a deep breath, and staying as calm as she possibly could, Sister Rosemary faced him and said, in his native Acholi, "What are you doing here? What do you want?"

"Sister, my gun is stuck. It won't work," he responded. "The government soldiers are nearby and they will catch me here. My comrades have gone and I want to leave too, but I have no working gun and I'm hungry. Do you have any food?"

Sister Rosemary found a small sack of groundnuts, scooping a handful and handing them to the man, along with a couple of potatoes.

"Thank you," he said, then hesitated. "Do you have any medicine?"

"Yes, what do you need?"

"Something for the pain."

Sister Rosemary left the room and when she came back, she handed the man two bottles, one full of aspirin and the other full of Panadol, a local brand of acetaminophen. "You must go away now, please," Sister Rosemary told him, noticing how young he was. "If the government soldiers find me helping you, we will all be in trouble. They will kill all of us."

The soldier picked up his broken gun and walked out. But before he was out of the school compound, he turned around and ran back to the kitchen building where he had been hiding before.

"Sister, I can't leave you in trouble like this."

She followed him, confused, and watched in shock as he opened the door of the wood-fired oven and began removing bullets from the ashes, and then from the flour that had been set out for the day's bread making.

"Before you walked in," he explained, "I put these in your oven. You have been good to me. I can't leave them here to blow up in your face."

By the time he had finished removing the bullets, it was clear that the soldier had concealed enough bullets to make the whole house explode the minute that she and the sisters began cooking dinner that night.

* * *

By 1988, Sister Rosemary had stopped attending classes. Outside the convent's walls the terror and the horrors continued. And the sisters persisted in providing refuge when needed to their suffering neighbors. When two medical students moved in with the sisters, Sister Rosemary dressed them in habits and veils.

"I'm not trying to get you to become sisters," she joked with them. "I'm just trying to protect you!"

Children without a Childhood

By far the most gruesome element regarding Kony's tactics was the fact that his militia increased their ranks by abducting children; according to some estimates as much as 60 percent of LRA insurgents were children under the age of sixteen. "These so-called child soldiers had been robbed of their childhood, held as captives by the LRA rebels, and forced into living nightmares," wrote Father Donald H. Dunson, a priest from the diocese of Cleveland and the author of *No Room at the Table: Earth's Most Vulnerable Children*. "After having been abducted, each of them was made to trek long distances between northern Uganda and southern Sudan laden down with stolen foods, goods, and arms. If they cried, they were beaten. If they cried again they were shot or their necks were broken with an iron bar. The female children were used as sex slaves, trophies given to the top officers in the LRA as rewards for military victories. Within the first three months of captivity, every boy was trained in the use of weapons and told that his gun was now 'his mother, his best friend, his everything.' These children were routinely used as human shields to protect the adults who were abusing and committing atrocities against them."

Father Don, who spent a considerable amount of time interviewing formerly abducted children who escaped and were living in a rehabilitation camp, explained,

> As I listened to former child soldiers tell me about how adults forced them to kill other children or to cut off another child's arm or leg solely because that child was slow, or stubborn, or sick, it was impossible for me to escape feeling some responsibility for the horrific ordeals inflicted on them. One teenager told me that another boy his age was killed by a rebel leader for simply eating meat on a day when they had been ordered not to. Some of the children were commanded to smear themselves with the blood of those who had been slain. Random cruelty is a way of life in the rebel group. . . .
>
> The rebels are experts in destroying bonds of trust and of love, especially the parental bond. Their objective is to get the children to believe that they belong to the rebel group, and the rebel group alone. In some extreme cases, rebel leaders have resorted to physically coercing the children into killing their own parents.[7]

And as the months pass, these children-turned-killers lose track of "their personal lives, their family culture and any kind of moral code. They learn indifference and brutality.

. . . Some escape. Some are rescued. Some are killed or die violently, as did 50 girls who drowned [in 2004] in the Moroto River. They had been forced into the river by the L.R.A. as they were running from the Ugandan army."[8]

For Sister Rosemary and the sisters at Sacred Heart Secondary School, the brutal conditions in Gulu finally became too much, and in 1989, the sisters made the decision to leave. Because looting in the area was so prevalent—and because they knew that the sisters who would come back to their school one day would need the furniture and things there, the women concocted a plan to hide things, basically in plain sight. One by one, the four sisters carried all the supplies, materials, and equipment they could hold and put them in a small room in the house. When the room was full, they locked the door and covered it up with plaster and bricks, painting the doorway the same color as the rest of the wall. Finally, they shoved a large piece of furniture in front of it.

After leaving the convent with only a few things in their possession, the sisters went to a deserted building a few miles away, part of a complex known as St. Monica's Girls Tailoring Centre. There they waited for a week—with no food—for the military escort that would take them to their motherhouse. What normally would be a long day's journey, however, turned into a whole week of travel as the military convoy transported passengers to various destinations in northern Uganda—finally delivering the four women to their motherhouse in Moyo.

An Expression of Love in the World

When Sister Rosemary and her three companions finally arrived safely at the community's motherhouse in Moyo, it was not immediately obvious to their fellow Sisters of the

Sacred Heart of Jesus just how much the previous three years in Gulu had changed them, all of them. Like all victims of tragic events or experiences, Sister Rosemary soon began to experience the effects of what mental health professionals now call post-traumatic stress disorder or PTSD. She was not sleeping well, often feeling jumpy or jittery. Darkness terrified her. She mechanically locked every door behind her. She found it impossible to relax, let alone feel safe. And she couldn't shake that sense of alertness that reminds a PTSD victim that anything can happen, at any time. No place—or moment—felt safe.

Sister Rosemary could have never guessed how the willingness and courage that she found deep inside her to face her own anxiety and fear would become one day the pillar of empathy with which she could help others—in particular, other women. She also could have never imagined then that, in reality, the horrors caused by the LRA were just beginning in their rule over northern Uganda.

In 1989, when Sister Rosemary was thirty-three years old, her community appointed her as first provincial superior over the Sacred Heart Sisters in Uganda and Kenya—a testament to their trust in her leadership, wisdom, and prayerful grounding. At first, however, Sister Rosemary hesitated, not feeling ready for such responsibility. But her trusted friend and advisor Father Luigi encouraged her to accept the position, affirming the community's decision and their request for her leadership. Sister Rosemary also eventually resumed her formal studies at a senior secondary school in the capital city of Kampala, Trinity College. Remaining in southern Uganda, two years later she earned an undergraduate degree in development studies and ethics from Uganda Martyrs University in Nkozi, fifty miles southwest of Kampala—followed by a master's degree in the same field.

Things settled down in the Moyo region, across the Nile river—where it was much more difficult for rebels to reach. By 1989, only a handful of refugees out of more than 300,000 were still in what was then one country known as Sudan and in Zaire (the modern-day Democratic Republic of the Congo). Most had gone back to their homes in Moyo and began rebuilding the area.[9]

In 1991, President Museveni began what appeared to be a coordinated attempt to eliminate the insurgency from the rest of northern Uganda. But the LRA rebel soldiers did not waste time before retaliating, stepping up human rights violations against civilians. In the early 1990s, for instance, dozens of LRA mutilation victims were referred to Lacor Hospital in Gulu after their lips, noses, and ears had been severed—with evidence that there were hundreds of other such victims unaccounted for.[10]

St. Pope John Paul II visited Uganda for six days in February 1993. At the Uganda Martyrs' Shrine, the pope emphasized words that proved to be prophetic for a country still at war with its own people:

> Truly the Uganda Martyrs became light in the Lord! Their sacrifice hastened the rebirth of the Church in Africa. In our own days, all Africa is being called to the light of Christ! Africa is being called again to discover her true identity in the light of faith in the Son of God. . . . All that is truly African, all that is true and good and noble in Africa's traditions and cultures, is meant to find its fulfillment in Christ! The Uganda Martyrs show this clearly: they were the truest of Africans, worthy heirs of the virtues of their ancestors. In embracing Jesus Christ, they opened the door of faith to their own people, so that the glory of the Lord could shine on Uganda, on Africa.[11]

St. John Paul II celebrated Mass in several regions, including one in the town of Gulu, where the pope's message was one of "hope and encouragement to a people troubled by years of insecurity and suffering. He rekindled the hope of the people as he reminded them of God's care and concern, as expressed in the figure of the Good Shepherd."[12]

The Worst of Humanity

The pope's visit created a lull in rebel activities that led to a relatively peaceful end of 1993 and beginning of 1994, when President Museveni gave the rebels who had been considering peace talks a seven-day ultimatum to surrender. The LRA responded by launching armed attacks, especially on roads, and by starting the widespread practice of planting land mines on both main roads and footpaths. One of these land mines detonated as late as 2015 just outside the walls of St. Monica's, where University of Oklahoma law students were staying as volunteers at the time. One woman was injured by the explosion, a prisoner from the women's prison across the street from St. Monica's who was doing work in the area.

During these years of great violence, there were many horrid "incidents" of mass murder and violence. But April 20, 1995, marks one of the most macabre of all events. The LRA marched into the trading village of Atiak and claimed unchallenged military control of the town, killing and attacking people for most of the day. While the exact number of victims is impossible to know, by the end of the day, as many as three hundred unarmed civilians had been killed—and dozens of children were abducted and taken into the bush.

A few months later, hundreds of rebel soldiers invaded the Kitgum district in northern Uganda and carried out a massive abduction of children and youth in order to beef up their forces. People in the Gulu district remember living for years in a world where the Lord's Resistance Army descended "to its worst depths of brutality. Civilians were killed or tortured almost everywhere on a daily basis and children were abducted [by] the thousands."[13]

Unable to control the situation, the government responded by beginning to move people away from their villages and into "camps," presumably for their safety. While it is true that some people went voluntarily, according to the document *Let My People Go: The Forgotten Plight of the People in the Displaced Camps in Acholi,* published by the Gulu Archdiocese in 2001, the majority of the people were "forced to move by Army personnel, who often used rather drastic methods. . . . Soldiers just stormed villages—often at dawn—without any previous warning. They told people to move immediately without giving them much time to collect their belongings. People were often beaten to force them out of their compounds. Much of the property left behind was looted by both rebels and soldiers. A number of people who ventured to go back to their former homes soon after found them burnt down. Men told us that they were harassed and even shot at, and women raped. A resident of Paicho [camp] summarized that experience of unbearable stress with these words: 'We were beaten by Government troops, who accused us of being rebel collaborators and told us to go to the trading centre. On the other hand, rebels would also come and threaten to kill us unless we moved deeper inside the bush.'"[14]

According to a 1997 United Nations report describing the "displaced people" situation, in the Gulu region, most of the district's population of 390,000 people were now living "in so-called 'protected villages.' According to figures from the local authorities, there are now 281,000 people living in 15 such sites around the district, a figure which includes resident populations and the displaced people who have joined them. . . . Politicians and soldiers are also on record as saying that the villages will be an important part of the [government's military] strategy to isolate the LRA and deny its members food, freedom of movement and the ability to re-group."[15]

* * *

Without developing a strong, durable root system, any plant, no matter how special its seed, would soon wither. The opposite also stands true. The larger the outward growth of a plant, the deeper that its root system must be. For Sister Rosemary, life was calmer in the late 1990s. She may not have known it then, but the years she spent in Moyo, followed by her time advancing her studies in southern Uganda, had provided her with critical knowledge and experience that would serve her well at her next assignment—as director of St. Monica's Tailoring School for Girls in Gulu.

Above all, this period in her life allowed Sister Rosemary the time, the experience, and the prayerful contemplation to grow deep, strong spiritual roots. It was a time of profound growth that—looking back on it now—prepared her for what has become the most important work of her life.

CHAPTER FOUR

With a Motherly Heart
(2001–2007)

Ask if this were merited; ask for its justification,
and see whether you will find any other answer but
sheer grace.

St. Augustine, Office of Readings,
December 24 (Sermon 185)

One of the first things people notice when driving into
the grounds of St. Monica's Girls Tailoring Centre is a giant
banyan tree, its powerful branches bursting out of the rich
red soil. Banyans, trees that can grow so big that they can
resemble a forest from afar, drop roots straight from their
branches. These roots can merge into stout pillars as thick
as English oaks—enabling them to grow longer branches
and send down even more roots. In India, the banyan tree
is a symbol of life and resurrection. At St. Monica's, the
banyan is a natural gathering place—and an appropriate
icon of resilience and hope. Roots can and will emerge as
new life bursts from the darkness. The tree's dark green
leathery leaves offer an umbrella-like protection from the

tropical sun or the abundant rain during the rainy seasons—and remind St. Monica's residents they do not have to walk alone. They can reach out and be shelter for one another.

The Comboni Missionary sisters founded St. Monica's school in 1983 as a vocational training center and boarding school for uneducated women in northern Uganda. In its early days, it was known as Adel School, in honor of the sister in charge, Sister Adeliana. Eventually, it was renamed after African-born St. Monica, the patron of wives and abused victims—and the mother made famous for her ardent prayers for her wayward son's conversion. St. Monica's son, Augustine, not only became a Christian, a priest, and a bishop, but also ultimately, a Doctor of the Church. The Comboni sisters handed over St. Monica's to the Archdiocese of Gulu in 2000. Soon thereafter the Gulu archdiocese entrusted St. Monica's to the Sisters of the Sacred Heart of Jesus. The school had seen better days. Only two barren classrooms were in use, leaving the U-shaped compound of buildings that could accommodate three hundred people mostly unused and in disrepair. Only two Sacred Heart Sisters taught tailoring classes to fewer than thirty students, and only one of the sisters could speak the girls' native Acholi, making it difficult to communicate with the students.

When Sister Rosemary was first asked to return to Gulu, she was honestly taken aback by this next assignment. She didn't know anything about sewing, but her reaction was not so much about being assigned to St. Monica's Tailoring School for Girls. She hesitated, in reality, because of the difficult and stark memories she still carried from her previous time in Gulu. It was 2001, and Gulu was hardly a stable environment. If anything, Kony and his Lord's Resistance Army continued to grow stronger, and their brutal attacks more frequent throughout the region.

"There have been many moments of making difficult deci-sions," notes Father Luigi, who has walked with Sister Rosemary as a constant companion, mentor, and spiritual guide over the years. At the time, "she struggled with the idea of being sent to St. Monica's. But I was certain that this is what she was called to do." Reminding her that her courage grows out of her deeply rooted spirituality, Father Luigi said to his friend, "Rosemary, this is the moment and you are the person to be there." Thinking back at that instant when he knew just what to say to her, Father Luigi recalls, "I don't know why . . . I can't really explain it, but I just knew this was right. Sometimes we don't like those things when we're going through them, but later on we know, we see."

The Unexpected Answers to Prayer

Even knowing that Father Luigi was right and trusting that it was the right decision, for Sister Rosemary saying yes to Gulu and St. Monica's was a legitimately difficult and chal-lenging moment. "I had already been in a bad situation there. I had been in Gulu when the war broke out!" she exclaims. When she was approached about her new assignment, "I had just come back to Moyo from completing my studies at uni-versity when they sent me back to Gulu," Sister Rosemary says, then pauses before adding thoughtfully, "I don't think the sisters understood the deep level of trauma that those of us who were trapped in the war went through—how scary it was. Trauma affects you deeply, deep in the body and deep in the spirit. It's very difficult to let other people really under-stand it and understand you at the same time."

In the end, Sister Rosemary acknowledges, it came down to obedience. "I always valued obedience in my life." This was one of those moments, she describes pensively, when "I knew that obeying even the most difficult situation would ultimately make me happy . . . and I go where God asks me to go." Yet again, as she reflects on it now, it proved downright providential that the Sisters of the Sacred Heart community discerned that Sister Rosemary was the strong leader who could forge a new direction for St. Monica's Girls Tailoring Centre.

But when Sister Rosemary arrived in Gulu in 2001, the physical condition of St. Monica's reflected the broken-down spirit of the Gulu community at large. People in the town of Gulu lived, at best, in daily insecurity and almost always in terror of what the LRA soldiers would do—and how the government would respond. It was a vicious circle with no apparent solution. The government army continued to offer the people of Gulu to move into "protected villages" for their security, according to a United Nations report outlining the humanitarian situation in Uganda. As usual, it was the civilians who were left in limbo.

In addition, the constant instability and uncertainty felt by the people of Gulu compromised the very livelihood of a culture overwhelmingly dependent on agriculture and cattle. "The recent insecurity has also undermined the ability of farm families to harvest their crops and prepare for the upcoming rainy season," stressed the UN report. Commenting on the situation at that time, the report cites as an example how "the [previous] harvest, which would have been a bumper crop due to good rains, rotted in the fields as farmers were too frightened to spend time on their land."[1]

"That was a difficult time," Sister Rosemary says, remembering how the attacks, death, and horrific injuries had all come to be expected as a daily fact of life in the region. Perhaps the most heartbreaking of all is the effect that the violence had on multiple generations of children in northern

Uganda. Kony's LRA soldiers continued to hunt children every night, storming into villages from the surrounding bush, kidnapping girls and boys as young as eight or nine from their homes, and forcing them to kill their own parents before marching them deep into the bush. Once they had the children in their possession, they brainwashed them into submission and into unwavering loyalty to Kony. During what became Africa's longest-running civil war, and because of the LRA's brutal and evil practices, northern Uganda was the only conflict in history where children were both the main victims and the principal aggressors.

In this world turned completely upside down, as many as forty thousand northern Ugandan children would seek safety from the attacks by leaving their parents every evening to go to "night shelters" protected by government troops.[2] The Gulu region was no different. Not having an answer or a way to defend themselves from the daily LRA raids on villages, about thirteen thousand people from neighboring villages entered the town of Gulu every evening to spend the night, hoping for added safety. Of those, the vast majority were children who were terrified of being abducted by the LRA. At St. Monica's alone, anywhere from three hundred to five hundred showed up each night, and Sister Rosemary and the sisters took in every one of the "nightwalkers," as they came to be known, hiding them from possible rebel assaults in any space possible, from storage closets to furniture.

"I was struggling so much with the children who we were hiding. We had nothing for feeding these children," Sister Rosemary remembers. With nowhere to turn for help, she reached out to her Comboni contacts in Italy who helped her find a source of aid. "I went to Rome, to the Community of Sant'Egidio, and begged them, 'Please help me to feed these children.' They immediately gave me money for food and to buy them mattresses, blankets, and other needs. I like to tell people, this is one organization that did not ask me for 'strategic plans' before helping me," Sister Rosemary says with a grin. "They simply responded. I love them for being a witness on how to care for the poor and the needy."

The Hand That Feeds You

It wasn't long after Sister Rosemary took over St. Monica's that an unexpected reality about the resident students got her attention. Some of the girls attending classes stood out. They seemed different, withdrawn, afraid to be noticed, unable to interact with their fellow students. One day, seizing an opportunity to be alone with one of the young women who seemed less withdrawn than the others, Sister Rosemary point-blank asked her about the cause for her behavior.

"I want to speak with you, Joy,"[3] Sister Rosemary began. "Why don't I see you talking to the other girls? Why won't you even look at anyone?" She paused, before adding, "What about me, can you look at me?" After waiting a while for a response, Sister Rosemary decided to try a different tactic. "Am I so ugly that you cannot look at me?" she joked, showing the girl her trademark smile.

The words surprised Joy and Sister Rosemary noticed a weak grin. "No, Sister Rosemary, you're not ugly."

"Then look at my eyes," Sister Rosemary said. "Tell me . . . why don't you talk to anyone, not even the other girls in the class?"

"Sister, I can't talk with them," Joy finally began. "I was with the rebels for nine years. I killed many people—and I am afraid the other girls will not understand."

This was the first time that Sister Rosemary pondered what it meant to have a girl at St. Monica's who was an actual "returnee," one who had been taken by the rebels and had escaped, and was now trying to integrate back into society. She had never thought about what this dynamic would be like for the returnee—or for the other girls at the school. Rather than "ex-soldier" or "victims," calling the children "returnees"[4] is meant as a neutral expression that incorporates both sides of their experience, as well as the community's encounter with them.

Children who either managed to escape on their own from the "kill or be killed" reality of living with the bush soldiers or were rescued from LRA camps often tried to go home, but most had no family to come home to and nowhere to go—or they were too damaged to naturally return to living in society. Some of the girls had been raped in front of their families before they were abducted. Others were taken, then forced to return to kill their families. All of them were trained to be killers and soldiers, and they were used as "wives" or given as prizes, sex slaves, for the LRA soldiers. In addition to being forced by their captors to witness, endure, and inflict unthinkable horrors on others, these are children who had been living for years without parents, without boundaries, without schooling, without a place to call home—without anything that resembles normalcy, safety, or personal support. Suddenly they found themselves "free," but without a family or any idea how to live or support themselves in a normal way in their culture. In addition, in Uganda's tribal culture, boys who escaped the LRA militia were able to return home and go to school. But girls who returned home—often arriving with their own children born of rape and violence, as well as with a host of sexually transmitted diseases—were rejected by their families, if they had any left, and shunned by the community.

After her conversation with Joy, Sister Rosemary began to take note of other girls who were acting in similar ways.

She then asked the other sisters to help her look for similar signs in other girls' behavior and to reach out to some of the girls they taught. What became quickly obvious to Sister Rosemary and the other sisters was that, in addition to the visible physical scars or deformities that the students bore from the violence they experienced in the bush—crooked knee joints, shattered jawbones, drooping eye sockets, missing earlobes—all the returnee girls, without exception, also carried deep and tragic wounds caused by the memories of the trauma they had experienced—and the violence they had been forced to inflict on others. And the more that the sisters learned about the girls and their background, the more the sisters realized there were many girls in a similar situation.

What, Sister Rosemary wondered at the time, could they do with and for these children? "You could see it in their faces," Sister Rosemary remembers, pausing, trying to describe what she was now well trained to recognize in the eyes of her girls. "They feel broken. They don't even trust anybody. And so you have to be patient, sometimes even be playful, before you can show them a place of happiness. That's the only way we can give them a chance."

Making matters worse, because most had been taken as young children, these girls had also missed out on any form of education. As the sisters began to hear their stories, it also became painfully clear that even the most basic vocational class, like learning how to sew, would be an insurmountable mountain to climb for girls who had never learned math. They simply had no understanding of numbers or measurements and how to use them, so Sister Rosemary began a literacy program for the girls, forming special groups for girls who shared this common past—but above all, girls who desired a new beginning but were lacking the building blocks of a basic education.

Within the vocational track, the sisters developed a separate curriculum for girls who were returnees and who were willing to learn how to sew using a practical, hands-on tailoring class—not from books or using math. To her surprise, as soon as she opened up the first hands-on class, ten of the thirty students at St. Monica's signed up. All ten, she eventually learned, had escaped life in the bush with Kony's soldiers.

Using only a tape measure and scissors, without patterns or math, the girls learned to estimate how much fabric to use and how to make a particular garment. Not long after that, Sister Rosemary and the other sisters added other basic classes, like cooking and baking, tracks that could also help the girls find practical jobs to support their families. And they made sure that the girls who needed it could have access to a day care for their little ones, the children fathered by their captors, so that both mothers and their children could together receive a St. Monica's education.

In reality, nothing could have prepared Sister Rosemary and the other sisters for this moment in their vocation. But in prayer and with resolve, they trusted that it was God who placed them in this place, at this time, with these children—and that God would make it clear to them how to reach these withdrawn, damaged girls who had become mothers not out of love, but out of violence, power, and force. One small decision at a time, they took care of the people and the needs as they were placed in front of them. How many more girls, they began to wonder, were in the same situation as those first ten St. Monica students? There was only one way to find out.

Over the radio, with printed flyers, even from the pulpit, the Sisters of the Sacred Heart began to invite all girls who had escaped captivity—and their children—to come to

St. Monica's. "We know there are girls out there who are interested in learning practical dressmaking and cutting. . . . St. Monica's welcomes all girls who came from captivity, all the child mothers who were forced to serve as soldiers alongside the rebels. Come as you are," the announcements read, "with your children, or even if you are pregnant. We'll take you no matter who you are, and give you the training you need to make a living. Registration starts in three days."[5] By the end of the year, two hundred girls had enrolled in the tailoring and catering classes at St. Monica's. No one was turned away.

Tortured Tales

"When I met Sunday, he was in the seventh week of his freedom, having been rescued by Ugandan security forces in a surprise ambush," writes Father Donald H. Dunson about one of his encounters with Uganda's returnees, a boy living in a rehabilitation camp. "Sunday has a bullet lodged in his leg, a souvenir of his eight-year captivity in the bush. . . . The emotional wounds he bears are far more serious. . . . His self-confident demeanor hides a most vulnerable adolescent. . . . Among the common side-effects that afflict formerly abducted children who have been brutalized in war are eating disorders, aggressive and militaristic behavior, epileptic fits, alcohol abuse, and the inability to form trusting relationships. Their terrorizing ordeals come back to them in flashbacks and nightmares. Many of the girls who escape bear the scourge of the sexually transmitted diseases with which they have been infected."[6]

According to Father Dunson, "Psychologists who have worked with former child soldiers suggest that acquiring a new and deep sense of belonging is the most crucial component to a successful reintegration process. Even though life will never be the same for these children and teenagers, even though there simply is no returning to the lives they knew before abduction, there can be healing."[7] Unfortunately, however, freedom often means exposure to negative experiences, where "former child soldiers are stigmatized through name calling and ridicule, often coming from their peers, whose acceptance they crave. Former child soldiers have heightened fears and are extraordinarily sensitive to any perceived sense of mistrust or avoidance. Their formal emotional development has been arrested as a result of the utter brutality they have known. . . . Knowing themselves to be different from their peers, they find the challenge of forming new friendships exceedingly daunting. Anxiety can even lead a few to ask, 'Why did I come back?'"[8]

One of the stories that Sister Rosemary will always carry in her heart and mind is about a twenty-year-old named Sharon,[9] who was thirteen when she was taken from her parents' home in the middle of the night by Kony's rebel soldiers, and who eventually managed to escape. After trying to make it on her own for five years, Sharon finally arrived at St. Monica's to live and learn skills to help her survive. She kept to herself, preferring to be alone rather than mingle with the other girls, even others who had also been held captive in the bush. "When she bent her head in the sunlight, the disfiguring outline of a burn scar glistened just beneath her dark, cropped hair. The inside of one forearm, from the wrist to the crook of her elbow, bore permanent stripes from a different kind of burn. She never smiled."[10] One day after classes, Sister Rosemary's prayerful intuition told her that it was time to approach Sharon and encourage her to tell her story. "Do you want to tell me what happened when you were living in the bush?"

Sister Rosemary began, keeping the question broad in order to give Sharon ample opportunity to say as much or as little as she could, but prepared to let it drop if Sharon wasn't ready.

"I can't," Sharon responded, staring at the ground. "You would never forgive me."

"Forgive you? Why would you need my forgiveness?"

"Because . . ." Sharon replied. Then she paused, taking in a deep breath before whispering out loud the words for the first time, "they made me kill my own sister."

When Sister Rosemary first realized the enormity of the situation, she felt helpless, she acknowledges, not knowing what to do. "Then you find out, the only thing you have which you can bring out is the little love you have in the heart—and then compassion is given. That opened my eyes, to accept them beyond what even they expected me to do." What St. Monica's became, no one could have ever predicted. The more Sister Rosemary and the community of sisters were present to the girls and their needs, the clearer the vision became, discerning piece by piece what next step needed to happen. The sisters even incorporated therapy into every vocational track they offered, an obvious but difficult aspect of the girls' rehabilitation and healing.

"When we open our arms and embrace these girls, they feel accepted. They become stronger and stand up straight!" Sister Rosemary says, smiling. Without a doubt, accepting unmarried mothers at St. Monica's was a new and unprecedented moment for the Sisters of the Sacred Heart of Jesus. But it was also an obvious extension of their ministry. "We knew our care had to include embracing both the mother and the child," says Sister Rosemary.

Being present to the girls, accepting them into the school and community as they are, demands a unique and insightful understanding of forgiveness in relation to God's love. "When I reflected about forgiveness, I thought of the prodigal son. This man, the father, accepted his son back and never asked him to give an account of the work, his life, where he'd been," explains Sister Rosemary. So every time she feels tempted to ask "Where have you been?" or "What did you do?" Sister Rosemary reminds herself, "*Rosemary, close your lips. The father of the prodigal son did not ask where his boy has been. Instead, he threw his arms around him, embraced him, gave him new clothes, new rings*. For me, that is a sign of life-giving—he gave life back to that boy."

The reality, Sister Rosemary adds, is that "we all have one of those in our lives! And the temptation of asking people about their past is what kills all of us. We ask, we want to know, how have you been using your money, how have you been living, where have you been—and really, we should all pray that God removes this desire to ask accountability of other people's lives. We want to hear him confess, hear her confess. It's like we are demeaning a person, humiliating them. That is not forgiveness or acceptance. When we open our arms and embrace them, they feel more accepted—they become stronger and stand up straight."

According to Sister Rosemary, she and the sisters learned much from that first group of girls at St. Monica's. Above all, walking with those girls helped the sisters to gain a clearer vision of their ministry to the suffering people of northern Uganda. They may not always know what they will be facing next, but the sisters learned how they would respond. This was to be their model. St. Monica's Girls Tailoring Centre would always welcome girls who had to drop out of school, girls who were taken into captivity, girls who became mothers by an act of violence and force—girls who had nowhere else to go. Working together and through the Lord's grace, the sisters vowed to become instruments for the girls' rehabilitation by showing them what genuine acceptance looks like, by walking with them as they are, and, above all, by being the presence of God's unconditional love for each one of them.

A Heart Aching for Her Kids

Late one warm night in June 2003, an LRA band of twelve soldiers jumped out of the northern Uganda tall grass and trees of the bush, surprising the residents of Adjumani, a small town approximately twenty-five miles south of what is now South Sudan. The soldiers moved silently through town, heading east, toward the Holy Redeemer Orphanage, run by the Sisters of the Sacred Heart. They stopped at the local parish to wake up Father Zachary, a member of the indigenous African community of the Apostles of Jesus. They roughed him up and ransacked Father Zachary's belongings before forcing him at gunpoint to walk them past the orphanage security.

One of the sisters woke up in the confusion and pleaded with them to stop, but the LRA soldiers—made up of kids and young adults between the ages of sixteen and twenty-five—forced the sister back into her room before abducting the orphans from their dormitories. They captured at least sixteen children, ages five to fifteen, nine of them girls, marching them out of the compound in a single file tied together with ropes. By now it was 2 a.m., and Father Zachary, who was at the end of the line and moving in pitch darkness, took a chance and slipped off into the bush to hide as the line of victims continued to move east. It was common knowledge that any adults taken with children by the LRA would be killed once they entered the bush. In a deranged initiation tactic, the newly abducted children would be given two choices: kill the adults or be killed.

That night, a very panicked Sister Joan called Sister Rosemary at St. Monica's in Gulu, asking for help, saying that she was following close behind the children who had been abducted, hoping to help them escape. "But the children were tied one after another, like slaves, and put in a trench," Sister Rosemary remembers, turning suddenly softer in both words and tone. "We managed to get some [government] soldiers to follow the children, but the children were being hidden by the rebels just along the roadside." That's when Sister Rosemary decided it was time to take a different approach.

"That very night I called Vatican Radio to tell them children were being abducted. And I called the International Refugee Trust because I had worked with them and I knew their number," Sister Rosemary says. "I told everyone I could about the children being abducted, and that way, the news went out internationally. I don't know how God instructed me to have enough sense to think all this through, but my hope was to scare some of the rebels not to kill some of the kids."

The next morning, Vatican Radio made an announcement about the abduction. The news went out immediately—"and I was being interviewed internationally, but I asked them not to mention my name because I am the heart of this program and they would come for me." One child was killed soon after being taken. He had epilepsy and could not walk. Sister Rosemary says, "The rebels said it was a bad omen and they killed him. These were children I had taken care of in Moyo before I went to Gulu. It was so painful. . . . We all started praying, asking St. Daniel Comboni to get back the children. Eventually, a good number of the kids were rescued."

For Sister Rosemary, the abduction of one particular child, the youngest in the group, hit her very hard. Five-year-old Francis had just been transferred to Adjumani from the orphanage in Moyo. "I had delivered Francis there myself," Sister Rosemary says seriously. "Francis was my boy. We'd go on walks and I'd say, 'Francis, you are big. . . . Carry the little ones on your back and follow me.' And he remembered all that I said. He was a very vivacious boy. When the rebels arrived, he was asleep. Awakened by the noise, he saw all of his companions standing in silence all tied up. And thinking it was a game, he asked to be tied up too, 'Take me! I want to go.' He didn't know where he was going. All I could think of was, now this boy is going to be killed. Can you imagine? It pained me so."

Months later, Sister Rosemary received a call from the army saying that two of the Adjumani orphans had been found near Kitgum. "These children gave my name to some soldiers, who then called me. I don't know how they even remembered my number. My God!" At first, Sister Rosemary was told that they would not release the children to her immediately. "But I told the army, no. I will go to pick them up right now." They had been separated and left behind by the rebels, the ten-year-old in Lira and the youngest of the abductees in Gulu, with a children's support group. "When I found Francis, he was playing around. Just looking at him, I felt like crying. When he saw me he said, 'Oh Sister, just today I was thinking, I hope I see one of my sisters.' I could not hold back my tears to see that boy. He had been with the rebels for about nine months."

In truth, Francis had changed. "He would look at me and then turn his head, as if rethinking where he was. I kept saying, 'Francis, I am the one. It is me.' I noticed that he had wounds on his body. I asked him what happened and he said, 'Sister, they used the starburst with a knife.'" Three months after the two boys were found, Sister Rosemary took them back to Moyo. "I asked the other orphans to make a cake for when they came home!"

Even now, so many years later, Sister Rosemary's voice changes as she remembers every detail in the stories about her children in Adjumani—the ones who were killed, like Patricia, who was caught trying to escape from the bush and shot, and the ones who made it. Some had escaped abduction by the bravery of Joseph, one of the older children. He was big enough and strong enough to pick up the kids and throw them out the window in order to protect them from being abducted by the LRA rebels. "Now he is a police officer in Sudan," Sister Rosemary notes proudly. Ultimately, however, "it was so traumatizing to leave the kids in Adjumani. They were just too scared." Not long after, the Sisters of the Sacred Heart moved the orphans from Adjumani to Moyo, turning the Adjumani facility into a grade school.

Oklahoma Meets Uganda

In November of 2003—the same year that former Ugandan dictator Idi Amin died in exile in Saudi Arabia—Oklahoma lawyer Reggie Whitten arrived for the first time to East Africa with a group of close friends. The trip organizer was J. Robert (Bob) Hunter, director of insurance for the Consumer Federation of America, based in Washington, DC. Bob and Reggie had met years earlier during a trial, when Reggie called on Bob to testify in a deposition, and the two men had become great friends over the years, having many things in common. It was not Bob's first time to Africa. He had been interested in helping the people of Uganda for years, even raising money in the United States for humanitarian projects in the northern region.

Nine months before arriving in Africa, Reggie Whitten had lived through every parent's worst nightmare, when his son Brandon was killed in a motorcycle accident caused by his addiction to drugs. Nothing prepares a parent for facing such a deep tragedy—and Reggie, understandably, had been suffering and depressed for months, reliving the grief of losing his son over and over again. That's when Bob and a common friend, Mike Hinkle, another Oklahoma lawyer whose kids had grown up with Brandon, finally stepped in. They were very concerned for the well-being of their grieving friend. After repeated conversations, Bob and Mike finally convinced Reggie to travel to Uganda, encouraging him with the promise, "It'll do you good. You need a change."

Bob Hunter, by coincidence that is clearly infused by God's Providence, had become a friend of Sister Rosemary's family over the course of his previous trips to Uganda. "I knew him through my sister Catherine," recalls Sister Rosemary. "He came to know me and always appreciated the work I was doing. It was Bob who decided to bring Reggie to Gulu." That is also how Bob decided that Reggie, after losing his son, would be better off to come and see Africa, says Sister Rosemary. "Reggie didn't want to come because he had had no contact with Africa."

On the multi-hour trip from Entebbe to Gulu, Bob narrated to Reggie the story of a nun who was helping the children of war-torn Gulu. He told his grieving friend about the LRA, how they kidnapped young girls and boys and how they indoctrinated them to become soldiers through fear, violence, and intimidation—and how these children were forced into committing the worst kind of horrors imaginable on other people, the kind of evil that only a miracle could heal. Above all, Bob described how this one particular woman named Sister Rosemary was making a difference, how she was slowly able to help these children who left the bush and who now had no way to know how to act, how to live, or how to make a life. To Reggie, the stories that Bob told him made Sister Rosemary sound like a super hero—perhaps even one too good to be true. But Reggie trusted his friends. And he had already been overcome with sadness for the needy children he could see as they drove north through the Uganda countryside.

Gulu in 2003 was a small town, "dotted with dilapidated, one-story structures. Young girls, no older than nine or ten years, carried babies on their backs, all of them orphaned by the war. The adults, unemployed and incapable of supporting themselves since the LRA conflict began terrorizing their town in the mid-1980s, propped their starving bodies against rundown houses and skinny tree trunks and stared at the car as it drove past. They shared the same hopeless look Whitten had only seen in pictures back home,"[11] a hopelessness perhaps similar to the one that Reggie had himself endured back in Oklahoma, overcome with grief and despair over his son's death. Reggie looked forward to finally meeting face-to-face the woman he had heard so much about, the woman whose love in action had put a dent into all the hopelessness around her.

When the three men finally arrived to Gulu and visited St. Monica's, however, Sister Rosemary was not there. She was away, traveling on school business. But what he and his friends encountered at the school nevertheless changed Reggie Whitten's life forever. "They found children, the night-walkers at St. Monica's," explains Sister Rosemary. And Reggie, focused on the pain of the children in front of him, was able, for a moment in time, to forget his own heartache.

However briefly, Reggie experienced a clearness he had not experienced for a while, and he vowed to return to Uganda. "He saw children that were suffering so much but who were able still to smile. Reggie could not believe it. It's what helped him make up his mind to help me!" Sister Rosemary says with a smile. "He went back home, and that's when he experienced a change in his heart and mind," allowing himself to move in a new and completely unexpected direction.

Some things in life change you forever, irrevocably altering the rhythm of your heart, the pattern of your spiritual DNA, that deepest ground that defines who you are. You don't get over or move past the death of a child, but you can learn that there is still life left inside you. What the trip to Uganda allowed Reggie to do was to learn to live again, not in spite of, but along with, the life-altering loss of his beloved son Brandon. After witnessing with his own eyes the deep scars carried by the children he met in Gulu, he, too, could find the strength to step through his own grief and focus instead on the pain that the children were suffering. He found himself wondering, *What allowed them to be able to still smile?* Back to work at his law practice in Oklahoma City, Reggie never stopped seeing in his heart's eyes the faces of the children he had met in Gulu. And as the weeks went by, he seriously pondered how, and what, he could do to help them.

A few months after his African pilgrimage, Reggie and his wife, Rachelle, traveled to Washington, DC, to attend the National Prayer Breakfast—and to finally meet Sister Rosemary in person. After the breakfast, the couple went to a reception at Bob Hunter's house, the home where Sister Rosemary was staying. It is funny to think about it now, but whatever image he previously had of the wonder woman from Gulu, Sister Rosemary was not it! She was much shorter than he would have pictured—and this person never stopped smiling. Joy, in fact, poured out with her every word, even when describing story after endless story of how she had stood up to soldiers threatening the safety of those under her protection. When Sister Rosemary spoke about the children—her girls—Reggie recognized in her expression the faithful and powerful love of a mother for her children. Whatever force was driving this woman in her work with those suffering children touched Reggie's heart so deeply that he and Rachelle immediately began to send Sister Rosemary donations. Being able to do something—even if it was just sending money—became for Reggie a healing and restorative experience. Nothing could make the pain in his heart from losing his son go away. But the idea that he could help Sister Rosemary in her work with these broken children changed his own gaze away from himself and toward someone else's needs. He began to realize, perhaps his life could make a difference after all.

When Sister Rosemary first met with Reggie, she thought to herself that he was a "simple person with a big heart," she says. "I didn't know how big he was [in his professional life]! He was very simple." Yet apart from all that Reggie Whitten has done to help Sister Rosemary over the years, she stresses, "Reggie became a good friend. His whole family became involved, and his wife, Rachelle, became a friend to me too." Stopping to emphasize her words, Sister Rosemary adds, "Reggie says meeting me saved his life. But also, meeting him has been a big event in my life too! And mind you, Reggie is not even Catholic. He says he grew up Baptist but doesn't take time to practice that. He believes strongly in me, someone who is not only a Catholic but also a Catholic nun, a religious! He believes in what I am doing," Sister Rosemary says, then pauses. "I think people [like Reggie] see God in practical things."

And it is those practical things that he has done so well—not only helping Sister Rosemary build her ministry and vocation to the young women in northern Uganda, but also making sure that everyone around the world could come to know Sister Rosemary and her vocation. This is the work that has changed Reggie's life forever.

* * *

In 2005, the International Criminal Court—the first permanent court to try individuals for genocides, war crimes, and other human rights violations—issued arrest warrants for five Lord's Resistance Army commanders, including Joseph Kony. It was the first time that a government state, Uganda, had asked the Hague-based court to investigate the LRA's practice of murder and torture during its nearly twenty years of fighting against the Ugandan army. A major aspect of the investigation centered on the LRA's practice of abducting children to become fighters and sex slaves, with the total number of children conservatively estimated in the thousands. Just one year later, the LRA began to move out of Uganda, with most of Kony's militants crossing the border into southern Sudan and the Democratic Republic of the Congo.

I Want to Thank the Sacred Heart of Jesus

On December 6, 2007, and in a very tangible way because of Reggie and Rachelle's efforts to make Sister Rosemary's work known in the United States, Sister Rosemary was awarded CNN's Hero Award. In a public statement acknowledging the honor, the Archdiocese of Gulu noted, the "Heroes award as a Community Crusader . . . is a great tribute to the work of Sister Rosemary, her community members the

Sacred Heart Sisters, and indeed the Archdiocese of Gulu in helping particularly girls in northern Uganda."

That evening, with a shaky, nervous voice, the woman who has stared down cobra snakes and gun-toting rebel soldiers in her native Uganda, stood up in New York City and declared,

> I want to thank the Sacred Heart of Jesus for this memorable occasion, which has extremely humbled me. Since 2003, I have been leading a Center which turned out to help young girls and women who have been victims of war. We decided to make the center a home to restore the lost dignity of the poor, young girls by helping them to love the children they got through violent experience from the rebel commanders.
>
> In humility and great gratitude I accept the CNN Heroes Award on behalf of these physically and psychologically traumatized young women and girls and children; and on behalf of the many people contributing like me to doing small things that are transforming people's lives. I honor the people working for justice and foundation for peace, as for reconciliation and the social re-construction of people's lives. . . . I want to say I honor the young women, the young mothers, who have been forced to become mothers before they were prepared. I receive this award on their behalf and I salute them all. And I want to say all this in the motto of our country—for God and my country. Thank you very much.[12]

CHAPTER FIVE

Love Is the Key! (2008–2017)

The greatest figures of prophecy and sanctity step
forth out of the darkest night. But for the most part,
the formative stream of the mystical life remains
invisible. Certainly the most decisive turning points
in world history are substantially co-determined by
souls whom no history book ever mentions. And
we will only find out about those souls to whom
we owe the decisive turning points in our personal
lives on the day when all that is hidden is revealed.

St. Teresa Benedicta of the Cross,
in Edith Stein, *The Hidden Life*

She stops to chat with a barefoot teenage girl and her
friend, each stitching away on a black, pedal Singer sewing
machine. The girls are sewing on a small porch outside their
classroom, hoping to take advantage of the cool Ugandan
afternoon breeze.

Something Sister Rosemary says makes the student smile.
The girl toys with the measuring tape hanging around her
neck, then hands Sister Rosemary the piece of material that

she'll be assembling into a shirt. It is clear as she looks over the student's fabric that Sister Rosemary is checking every detail with utmost attention. She is blunt but kind in her remarks to the teenager, who responds with a serious, "Yes, Sister. I understand, Sister. Thank you, Sister," before once again smiling at Sister Rosemary's final words.

Sister Rosemary Nyirumbe knows very well how essential it is for her girls to have pride in their work and in themselves, not only in spite of, but also because of, the obstacles and suffering they've endured. "We want these girls to know they are worth something. They are not begging or asking for money. They are learning a trade," she says, then stops and pauses for a moment to emphasize this fact. "It is very important to have girls educated in order for them to be able to meet the challenges of the world tomorrow."

In practical, feasible ways, in her work with returnee girls—as well as others unwanted because of their past—Sister Rosemary seeks to replenish the emptiness and hollowness left within each girl's spirit. The broken vessels they had become, she could not put back together. But she knew from her own experience that trusting God's path for her life had always given her the strength to walk and live through moments she never thought she'd be able to survive. Rooted in prayer, graced by love, Sister Rosemary was, even now, living an indescribable reality in her pastoral work. Yet she has trusted that, as long as she does her part, giving herself to each moment in front of her, God always takes the puzzle and makes the pieces fit together.

As a result, she helped the returnee girls learn how to sew, even though they lacked a formal education. She created a literacy program, teaching many of them how to read and write. She trained the girls in practical and vocational skills, from cooking and cleaning to manners and child care. She educated their bodies, counseled their damaged minds, and, above all, became healing balm for their spirits. Sister Rosemary's vision for how she and the other sisters could minister to these broken girls at St. Monica's school was to meet them, be present to them, love them—right where they were, and as they were. And in so doing, the Sisters of the Sacred Heart of Jesus became an antidote to the poison that had been injected into the girls' veins by the Lord's Resistance Army. The LRA tactics had undeniably done heavy damage in the quest to break them, to destroy each child's human dignity by forcing them to do the inhumane. But Sister Rosemary is the cure, and her secret weapon is love rooted in presence.

Journalist Patricia Smith will never forget one such moment that she was graced to witness. A freelance writer and photographer, Patricia has traveled to Uganda several times to report on Sister Rosemary's work.[1] On one of her visits to the Moyo orphanage, a teenage girl came to greet Sister Rosemary when their group arrived, but rather than walk up to her, the girl, "sat on the floor and would never raise her eyes to meet Sister's eyes," remembers Patricia. "Sister told her to look at her . . . then she asked her, 'Do you not think that you are beautiful?' The young girl shook her head no, and put her head back down." Sister Rosemary asked the girl the same question a couple of times, always getting the same reply. "Then Sister Rosemary turned to me and asked me to get my mirror compact," says Patricia, smiling, "Sister knew I brought it with me all the time. . . . I had learned from previous visits that mirrors were sometimes a luxury in Uganda! Sister opened the mirror and told the young lady to look at herself, saying over and over 'You are beautiful!'" Patricia recalls, with tears in her eyes. "We all started crying tears of joy. The young lady had the biggest smile, with tears running down her face. Sister made her a believer in her own inner and outer beauty!"

More than any awards or honorary degrees, what Patricia says she respects and admires most about Sister Rosemary is "her heart to serve. I love her heart and spirit. I love seeing her energy—when everyone has tired out. I love her smile and her giggle when she is happy. She is godly, spiritual, kind, motherly, unselfish, intelligent, and tough. She represents, leads by example, and shares the love of God. She is short in stature but is the tallest in her relationship with God!" describes Patricia, who after visiting Uganda became a volunteer for the Sewing Hope Foundation.

Much like her favorite Scripture, 1 Corinthians 13, Sister Rosemary says it is critical we recognize that all—and any—work we do is for nothing, if we don't have love. "Real love will always make you different. I totally believe that with love, you can have so many doors open," Sister Rosemary explains. "In order for me to do anything," she stresses, "I really need to develop love—because without love, I just can't do it. It is love that opens my arms and my heart."

In ministering to people whose background is really difficult, like the girls at St. Monica's, concedes Sister Rosemary, "I would be scared. I would not be able to accept them . . . if I didn't have love. When we open our arms and embrace [the girls], they feel more accepted—they become stronger and stand up straight. You can see the change, physically. And that's why I say, it is love which is the key for doing all the work we can do!" Affirming a truth that crosses boundaries of time and geography, the woman who has been described as the Mother Teresa of Africa proclaims, "I have treasured 1 Corinthians 13 for many years. Love, if I don't have it . . . what happens?"

Standing Up for Her Girls

By 2008, Sister Rosemary had become proficient at finding creative ways to fund her ideas and the many programs at St. Monica's carried out by the sisters. For example, when her older sister Catherine, who was at the time serving as a state minister of public service, called her about finding a driver to take her places in Gulu while she attended a conference, Sister Rosemary did not hesitate to volunteer for the job. "I'll drive you!" she said, with the attitude that every little bit makes a difference. Using the money she earned serving as Catherine's driver, the equivalent of 100 US dollars, Sister Rosemary was able to get help cleaning up the grounds at St. Monica's, making the place more welcoming for visitors—and more beautiful for their resident students.

Whatever the problem that presented itself, Sister Rosemary was always thinking of ideas—often out loud—on how to find a solution. When it was obvious that the number of young children being brought to St. Monica's required a daycare, she sought the aid of a Spanish priest who helped her acquire five thousand euros for the building's construction. When the number of children outgrew the small daycare, one of her friends at the Dutch embassy sent the ambassador to check out the sisters' work at St. Monica's. "You have a lot going on in your compound," the woman told Sister Rosemary. "But what are your priorities for next year?" Moved by what she had seen, the ambassador approved Sister Rosemary's verbal request for funds for an expanded nursery and daycare.[2]

During this time, soldiers with the Lord's Resistance Army continued their evil fear tactics, in spite of international pressure weakening their forces. In Gulu, even during periods of calmness and relative peace, the population continued to suffer community-wide anxiety underlying all "normal" activity. The unspoken question on everyone's mind remained—when and where would the LRA pop its snakehead up next?

One afternoon at St. Monica's, Sister Rosemary was surprised to find a group of girls kneeling at the feet of an LRA commander who had strutted into the school compound, clearly acting as if the girls still "belonged" to him.

"Excuse me, sir," Sister Rosemary interrupted the group. "I'm asking you to kindly not come on this compound again," she continued, without hesitation.

At first, the officer snickered in reply.

"You make these girls feel like they are back in the bush, like they have to be loyal to you," Sister Rosemary boldly stated. "They are different now. They don't answer to you," she said, pausing for emphasis. "Will you leave now? Can you do this for me?"

The soldier stared at Sister Rosemary, who was not backing down, before finally replying, "Okay, Sister, okay. Whatever you say."[3]

Even after the LRA rebel forces were forced north, crossing into South Sudan, a number of LRA commanders returned to northern Uganda wanting to reclaim their bush "wives." One day at St. Monica's, Sister Rosemary found herself face-to-face with one such visitor who entered the building that held her office.

"I have come to collect my wife. Her name is Amelia," said the young officer, standing in the doorway in such a way that there was no possible way for Sister Rosemary to exit past him.

"You have a wife here?" Sister Rosemary asked, praying silently for the right words to use in talking with him.

"Yes, and I want her back."

"Did you marry the girl you say is your wife?" Sister Rosemary inquired.

"No, but when we were in the bush, we were staying together. Now . . . where is she?"

Without allowing even one moment of hesitation, Sister Rosemary countered, "Staying together is different from being married. Tell me, did you traditionally marry her? Did you pay the bride price, as is customary?"

"No," he countered, "but her parents say I can stay with her now, in the village."

There were many things going through Sister Rosemary's mind all at once as the young soldier continued his aggressive interrogation. But the most important one was a simple prayer, straight from her heart, "*Please, don't let Amelia show up while we are talking. Please protect her.*"

"That is not marriage," Sister Rosemary answered, looking straight at him. "You used her when you were in the bush, against her will, and that is not marriage. So I'm asking you to get out and leave this place. . . . You are not taking her with you. You have no wife here. You can go your way now."

Sister Rosemary knew that this encounter could easily escalate and blow up in her face, but by the grace of God, her voice remained as calm as was humanly possible, as she continued to look at the soldier's eyes. Finally, mumbling something under his breath, the soldier turned around and left the building, then continued walking out of the St. Monica compound.

In December 2008, the military forces of Uganda, the Democratic Republic of the Congo, and southern Sudan launched a joint operation against the Lord's Resistance Army's camps located in northeastern Congo. Not only did the operation fail to apprehend Joseph Kony, but his forces retaliated with a series of attacks and massacres in Congo and southern Sudan, killing an estimated nine hundred people in two months alone. The instability and violence was making news all over the world almost daily.

It wasn't long before the US Congress joined international efforts against Kony and his militia, proposing what came to be known as the "Lord's Resistance Army Disarmament and Northern Uganda Recovery Act of 2009," which cited among its factors the following:

> For over 2 decades, the Government of Uganda engaged in an armed conflict with the Lord's Resistance Army (LRA) in northern Uganda that led to the internal displacement of more than 2,000,000 Ugandans from their homes.
>
> The members of the Lord's Resistance Army used brutal tactics in northern Uganda, including mutilating, abducting and forcing individuals into sexual servitude and forcing a large number of children and youth in Uganda, estimated by the Survey for War Affected Youth to be over 66,000, to fight as part of the rebel force.
>
> According to the United Nations Office for the Coordination of Humanitarian Relief and the United Nations High Commissioner for Refugees, the new activity of the Lord's Resistance Army in northeastern Congo and southern Sudan since September 2008 has led to the abduction of at least 1,500 civilians, including hundreds of children, and the displacement of more than 540,000 people.[4]

In addition, the Northern Uganda Recovery Act of 2009 made it US policy to kill or capture Joseph Kony and to finally, after decades of existence, crush Kony's Lord's Resistance Army rebellion—as a means of promoting and pursuing the security and stability of the people of central Africa. President Barack Obama supported the initiative, announcing that he would deploy one hundred US military advisors to Uganda, southern Sudan, the Central African Republic, and the Democratic Republic of the Congo to help the regional forces. The US military personnel, however, were not authorized to fight unless they were fired upon. Nevertheless, the armed international pressure succeeded in forcing Kony's troops out of Uganda, spreading them throughout the lawless territories bordering the regions of the Central African Republic, South Sudan, Sudan, and the Democratic Republic of the Congo. In a congressional hearing in October 2011, a deputy of the US Bureau of African Affairs declared that the US remained committed in efforts "to promote comprehensive reconstruction, transitional justice, and reconciliation in northern Uganda."[5] Yet in spite of all the international efforts, Joseph Kony evaded capture—and, in fact, has never been apprehended.

A Second St. Monica's

According to the United Nations Refugee Agency (UNHCR), at the peak of the war between the Ugandan army and the rebel forces of the Lord's Resistance Army in the mid-2000s, there were 1.84 million internally displaced people (IDPs) living in 251 camps across 11 districts of northern Uganda. After the cease-fire agreement of 2006–2007, almost all IDPs returned to their villages to rebuild their homes.[6] From its Gulu office, the UNHCR agency helped an additional 11,600 of the most vulnerable internally displaced people to either return home or to integrate where they were. This involved resolving land issues, building huts and latrines for needy individuals, and providing a start-up kit and support safety net in the form of blankets, kitchen sets, livestock, seeds, and tools. As time went by,

northern Uganda began the long and slow process of re-
claiming its culture, resettling its citizens, and healing—or
rather, trying to heal—the deep and violent wounds of its
people.

St. Monica's Girls Tailoring Centre continued to play a
critical role in the healing process, especially as countless
girls continued to escape from the bush after spending years
with the warlord's armed forces. It was clear to Sister
Rosemary that their ministry was not only still relevant and
significant, but also, in this new way, was just beginning.
"These girls had experienced unspeakable things," Sister
Rosemary emphasized. So many had been raped in front of
their families before being taken into the bush. Others were
taken without much violence, only to be brought back to
their villages and forced to kill their parents or siblings. All
of the girls arriving at St. Monica's after escaping from the
bush had been used as sex slaves and trained as soldiers.
Their trauma was often visible, their scars telling the tales
that many simply could not verbalize. Yet with patience,
prayer, and all the grace available to them, the Sacred Heart
Sisters continued to pour love on each girl, helping her believe that there was, indeed, a future life available to her—
and to her children.

Every month, more girls showed up at St. Monica's—many
of whom had traveled a considerable distance to arrive in
Gulu. The fact that a large number of girls came from the
regions north of Gulu gave Sister Rosemary an idea. Rather
than figure out how to transport these girls to St. Monica's,
what if they could start another St. Monica campus farther
north? "It all began when we realized there were too many
women in Atiak to uproot and take to Gulu, so we started
vocational training there—thanks to the CNN award money
and a substantial donation from Reggie and others in Okla-

homa," Sister Rosemary explains. "It began as a replica of Gulu, but it grew to become even more."

Located on the primary trade route between Uganda and South Sudan (only twenty-two miles south of the border), what is now called Sewing Hope Children's Village began in 2009 as a vocational school—a second St. Monica's campus—for girls from the far north region. At first the sisters worked with the local parish at Atiak, using the parish facilities with eyes toward building at a separate site. The fact that the new campus is located near the site of the scandalous Atiak massacre is not lost on Sister Rosemary. In a genuine way, she says, "It is an act of hope" and tremendous courage, to establish a village fueled with love near the site where Kony's Lord's Resistance Army executed by gunfire approximately three hundred civilians and kidnapped hundreds of young children—one of the ghastliest attacks in the decades-long LRA rebel war.

Sewing Hope

During this time, Reggie Whitten continued to support Sister Rosemary by sending money from Oklahoma and making personal visits, all the while discerning how to partner with St. Monica's and help it grow. Not only did Reggie and Rachelle Whitten become St. Monica's primary benefactors, more importantly, their friendship with Sister Rosemary grew, thanks to email, cell phone calls, and many in-person visits. During one of Sister Rosemary's visits to Oklahoma, Reggie decided it was time to make Sister Rosemary's story and her message heard at a national and international level. He began at first by making arrangements for Sister Rosemary to speak at local universities and other national venues during her visits. Being the practical and realistic lawyer that he is, Reggie also knew that this new African initiative had to have a recognizable theme and face, and that it needed to become something that would continue long after he and Rachelle were gone.

The name Pros for Africa, as the initiative was tagged, reflects its purpose as an organization made up of professional volunteers of every kind—doctors, dentists, engineers, teachers, lawyers—all people and services willing to help Sister Rosemary and the other sisters in their ministry. Reggie also recruited the help of some of his friends with sports connections, people who could make his vision for helping Sister Rosemary known to big-name athletes who'd be willing to contribute financially, but who could also provide national publicity and attention to their cause.

But Reggie did not deceive the millionaire athletes with a super rosy picture of what a possible Uganda adventure would entail, should they choose to participate.

> The trip to Africa, he told them honestly, would be rough—no five-star hotels, no luxurious beaches, no nightlife. Getting there would take more than twenty-four hours via an oceanic journey to Paris or London, followed by a daylong flight to Entebbe and a grueling four-hour drive to Gulu. They would have to avoid drinking the water, sleep under mosquito nets, and accept the fact that the phone service would probably be unreliable. Before the trip, they would need seven or eight vaccinations; afterward, it might take them a week to recover from the jet lag and lack of sleep. And they would have to pay their own way. "Oh," Whitten added, "you'll be physically working your butts off, digging and building things and handing out food to people who don't speak your language."[7]

The list of professionals who were not afraid of this challenging experience grew. And in March 2010, the first group of Pros for Africa—forty-eight volunteers in all—arrived in Uganda, and Sister Rosemary was there to welcome them.

"At the very beginning, Reggie was supporting us financially from his family money, from his pocket. He and Rachelle did a lot of that. But he always said this organization has to live past all of us, when we are not here," Sister Rosemary explains about Pros for Africa. "From the beginning he involved famous people, like the athletes." The CNN Hero Award, Sister Rosemary notes, also contributed to her mission because it came with prize money. But Reggie and Rachelle never stopped contributing from their own funds. When she told Reggie of the amount of the prize money from CNN, "He said to me, you need much more than that—and so he tripled the amount!"

Along with the doctors, dentists, water-well engineers, lawyers, teachers, and students who traveled with Pros for Africa those early years, volunteers also included NFL players Tommie Harris, Adrian Peterson, Larry Fitzgerald, Quinton Carter, Roy Williams, Mark Clayton, and Gerald McCoy. But at St. Monica's there was no distinction made between superstar athletes and other professionals. The real showcase was their result. Under the direction of Water4 volunteers, that first Pros for Africa group drilled one water well and broke ground for five more at various sites, including at St. Monica's, at Sister Rosemary's home village of Paidha, and at Restore Leadership Academy, a nearby school for boys—most of them orphans—founded by humanitarian lawyer Bob Goff in 2007.

That first Pros for Africa group also included a young and talented filmmaker named Derek Watson who had just started his own company, Lampstand Media. It was obvious to Derek from the beginning what a gem Sister Rosemary is—and what a wonderful story hers was to tell. So telling the story of northern Uganda and Sister Rosemary's vocation at St. Monica's became Lampstand Media's very first project. That Uganda assignment resulted in not one, but two, award-winning documentary films by Derek and Lampstand Media: *This Is Normal*, about Water4's mission of equipping people in developing nations with the means to eradicate their own water crisis; and the second, *Sewing Hope*, about Sister Rosemary and her school for girls. Both films won prizes. *Sewing Hope*, Derek's feature-length documentary narrated by Academy Award–winning actor Forest Whitaker, was selected by numerous film festivals around the world, including the Napa Valley Film Festival, the Sarasota Film Festival, the Toronto Black Film Festival, Richmond International Film Festival, and the San Luis Obispo Film Festival.

The name Sewing Hope comes, of course, from sewing being one of the vocations taught at St. Monica's. Over time, it also came to reference, in particular, handbags made by the St. Monica girls from recycled material—soda can pop tabs stitched together—that Sister Rosemary sells even now on her travels around the world. "Turning waste into beauty, we help the girls re-stitch a life that was thrown away, helping them see it as beautiful once again," says Sister Rosemary, pointing out that "Sewing Hope" is much more than a symbol. Every time a bag is made, she explains, "We witness how these girls learn self-confidence" and how they have learned to provide financially for their own families.

Her ministry is tough and full of incredibly difficult days, notes filmmaker Derek Watson, who describes Sister Rosemary as bold, visionary, loving, fearless, and, most of all, Christ-like. "When you meet her, you know you're meeting someone special and unique. . . . She 'saw' me, and by her nature, I think she 'sees' everyone. She is also just fun. I laugh so hard when I'm with her!" exclaims the thirty-four-year-old award-winning director. "She has purpose. You look into those eyes and you know there are thousands of stories in them and you want to sit at her feet and listen to them all," adds Derek. "She works with people who have higher needs than most of us in the West could even comprehend. It's not just poverty but social and cultural oppression and scars that run generations deep because of the conflict in northern Uganda. . . . We are all broken, but she has a way of making you feel at ease with that, which is why she's able to help some of the most scarred and oppressed individuals who have walked this earth. Her attitude and presence is how she brings healing, through the love of Christ, to so many."

Since they first met in Gulu back in 2010, Derek's admiration for Sister Rosemary has only grown. "She sees people as being created in the image of God. She sees their brokenness and also the beauty that God sees in them at the same time. It is truly inspiring to witness!" Remembering some of the inevitably long eighteen- to twenty-hour workdays they have shared together, Derek says, "It is difficult work. You can tell some days it truly does impact her. But she allows herself to be replenished by the Holy Spirit, and the love of Christ fuels her when she has given it her all."

One of the things that has impressed the Oklahoma-based filmmaker the most has been to witness how Sister Rosemary is "the same in every situation, from movie premieres, galas, talk shows, dinners, down to her everyday work." He explains, "I've seen her interact with world leaders, influencers, movie stars, star athletes . . . individuals that our society would deem as the elite or the highest echelon of power and influence. I've also seen her interact and love the most 'powerless' that this world has . . . orphans in the bush, the poorest of the poor, the sick, the elderly, the absolute destitute—all with the same amount of love and dignity that she shows a Madeleine Albright or Bill Clinton."

While she can handle being in the presence of presidents, professional athletes, kings, or bishops, and she has faced more than one snake in her lifetime, there is one thing that Sister Rosemary fears with all her might—and that brings her to a complete halt, or to run away like a scared animal—caterpillars!

One day, Sister Rosemary was at St. Monica's working with a woman, along with Sister Rufina and the Bishop of Sudan, who was visiting. "I looked at the woman, who had a caterpillar on her chest, and I started screaming and running away! The poor woman started running after me, wondering what was going on," recalls Sister Rosemary with a tone of voice that is both serious and full of concern. "I kept yelling at Sister Rufina, saying, 'Please, PLEASE, tell her in her language that she has a caterpillar on her chest!'—but I never stopped running," admits Sister Rosemary. "I am just terrified of caterpillars. I have prayed that this fear go away, but so far . . ."

"We Must Become Mothers"

Sister Rosemary knows a lot about mothering, and it's not just the nuts and bolts of how to change a diaper or console a crying child. She has felt, and acknowledges, how motherhood stretches a woman's heart much farther than anyone—including herself—thinks is humanly possible. She has firsthand experience of how a mother's heart incorporates each child's heart and makes it part of her own. She is familiar with the understanding that allows a mother to, literally, feel along with the child—her pain, her sorrow, her joy, her anxiety, her fear, her regret, her forgiveness, her hope, her healing—and in so doing, to hold her and all of it within the truth of love. She also knows tough love, when a mother is the only one who can be brutally honest when the situation calls for it. Sister Rosemary knows, because she has experienced it over and over, the heart-wrenching, worrisome, wonderful reality of a mother's heart.

While some of her mothering is intuitive and a gift from the Holy Spirit, Sister Rosemary has also chosen the path of spiritual motherhood, for herself and for sisters. Early on in her work with the girls at St. Monica's, it was clear that what they needed was a mother's love. And when the number of returnee girls grew, and they showed up at St. Monica's doorstep with children of their own, Sister Rosemary knew without a doubt that what she and the sisters had to do was become mothers to the girls. "We must help these girls learn to love the children they had with rebel soldiers," she told the other sisters at St. Monica's. "We must become more . . . we must become mothers to these girls. Let us be kind to them in order for them to be kind to others. That's what God wants us to do."[8]

Reggie Whitten knew that, from the time he first met her, Sister Rosemary's story was one that needed to be told. And in early 2013, Reggie did just that, publishing the book *Sewing Hope,* co-authored with journalist Nancy Henderson. The book tells the story of Sister Rosemary Nyirumbe in relation to Joseph Kony and his impact on the people of northern Uganda. With a picture of Sister Rosemary on the cover, the book's subtitle states, "Joseph Kony tore these girls' lives apart. Can she stitch them back together?"

"It is essential that the eyes of the world remain on Uganda and South Sudan," wrote Reggie in the book's afterword. "These children of the war must never be forgotten, lest history follow in the footsteps of tyrants once again. The schools created and maintained by Sister Rosemary are building young lives that will change the world in a good way. She is raising young women up to stand on her shoulders. She is indeed deserving of the Nobel Peace Prize as anyone who has ever earned that great honor," noting that he dreams of a day when she'll be nominated for that award. "But she will not hear of awards or accolades, for her work continues. Every day, it's a challenge to keep her school open and running. . . . Telling this story has been a long journey undertaken by my friends and fellow volunteers at Pros for Africa, but we now have the story in book and movie form. Now we can only hope everyone gets a chance to see and hear it."[9]

A year later, in 2014, Sister Rosemary was recognized as one of the "100 Most Influential People" in the world by *Time* magazine—an honor she shared that year with Pope Francis. Her bio, written and presented by producer, director, and Academy Award–winning actor Forest Whitaker, noted,

In Gulu, Uganda, Sister Rosemary has made it her mission to provide within an orphanage a home, a shelter for women and girls whose lives have been shattered by violence, rape and sexual exploitation.

At the Saint Monica Girls' Tailoring Center she runs, those women can become themselves again, thanks to the security and comfort they feel—a tremendous accomplishment in a country still fragile from years of civil war. But what truly fascinates the people who have the privilege to meet with Sister Rosemary—as I did when I narrated a film about her, *Sewing Hope*—is her magnetic and contagious energy.

For girls who were forcibly enlisted as child soldiers, Sister Rosemary has the power to rekindle a bright light in eyes long gone blank. For women with unwanted children born out of conflict, she allows them to become loving mothers at last.

The traumas she heals are unfathomable, but the reach of her love is boundless.

As she stood in front of hundreds of award winners and dignitaries, Sister Rosemary's words that night remained focused on her girls. "I'm going to talk as a mother," she remarked. "I took these children in, that's why I became a mother—to teach them to love, to teach them that life does not end in pain and that their future cannot be defined with the conflict, or by the pain they went through," she said, before pausing. "I told them to go above their pain. They are using the needle and sewing machine to fight back—and these women are great winners, they are victorious. They have won their battle—they are above the rebels. The women," continued Sister Rosemary, "are walking with their heads up in dignity. They are able to love. They are able to teach us ALL how to love!"[10] That same year, Sister Rosemary received the United Nations Women's Impact Award.

And in May 2014 a video clip of her interview with Stephen Colbert became a social media sensation as perhaps the only documented instance on television of a nun threatening to punch someone. She was invited to Comedy Central's *The Colbert Report* show to discuss the effectiveness of hashtag activism in the wake of the #BringbackourGirls campaign—the 276 schoolgirls kidnapped from a Nigerian secondary school in Chibok by Boko Haram terrorists. When asked, "Is hashtag activism a good thing or a bad thing?" by Colbert, Sister Rosemary unequivocally responded, "It's the best we can do. We haven't done enough! We should continue shouting . . . we must shout #BringbackourGirls! It happens very often, but we keep silent about it," she emphasized. "The world is silent about it. It happens all over the world. It is a global problem. That's why I'm here, reminding people . . . reminding ourselves, we've got to shout about it and bring an end to this." Yet when Colbert, in his best bully impersonation, mockingly asked why he should care about a situation in Africa that makes him sad and it's a long way away—thousands of miles away—when there are things at home to be sad about, Sister Rosemary looked him in the eye and waved her fists as she replied, "If you cannot be sad because it is happening in Africa, which is part of the humanity, I would feel like jabbing you."

"Really . . . You, a nun, would punch me?"

"Yeah, yeah I would. I would jab you!"

Colbert challenged, "Am I allowed to punch you back?"

"No," she said firmly.

"How's that fair?"

"Because I am going to punch you and I will win," she concluded, to the delight of a cheering audience.[11] A few months later, a follow-up YouTube video attempted to continue the conversation with Colbert, himself a winner of *Time* magazine's 100 Most Influential People. The video jokingly showed Sister Rosemary in training with American boxer Terence Crawford, who was at the time lightweight champion of the world, as she publicly challenged Stephen Colbert to a future match in Uganda. "I am challenging Colbert to come, not only to Uganda, but to Gulu. . . . And to show you that I am serious about punching you, I have a secret trainer." The video ended with a public challenge for the television host, "Colbert, do you accept the challenge to come to Africa?"[12] But to this day there has been no reply.

It is safe to say that Sister Rosemary will do just about anything, including employing good-natured jabbing, to bring the plight of her girls to light for the world to know—and specifically, to make Americans conscious of those who suffer thousands of miles away on the other side of the earth, no matter how much sadness it may bring.

A Light in the Darkness

In 2016, Sister Rosemary was awarded the inaugural John Paul II *Veritatis Splendor* Award by the Malopolskie Voivodeship assembly. In announcing the award, they noted,

> The sister's actions and work are an ideal reflection of St. John Paul II's teachings in his *Veritatis Splendor* encyclical. The joyful truth of Christian faith, to which she owes her deeply humane character and unusual straightforward manner, makes her the ideal candidate for this award. She not only lives in the "light of truth," but gives the gift of herself to girls who are excluded from society and marginalized. Sister Rosemary has wisely and consistently interpreted the evangelical obligation to love thy neighbour; for these abandoned women, she is not only a teacher, but, more importantly, a mother. She not only gives them a literal roof over their heads and food on their plates, but something much more: she sees in them the exceptional dignity of a human person, and discovers in them the real humanity of mankind. There are very few who can protect the girls' inner goodness and see the image of God in their tired faces. Her love and devotion are the result of her serious approach to her calling.

In her response to the award, Sister Rosemary said about herself, "I am not here to speak or cry out about the pain of these women. It can no longer be an option for us, but an obligation to become engaged in healing the world of these women, in order to allow them to stride in hope towards a better tomorrow! I ask each person of influence in the world to help heal the world together, starting from a single woman, from a single child."[13]

CHAPTER SIX

The Genius of Woman (2018–)

I want the world to know about her sincerity, that
it is grounded in a real love of the Risen Christ. She
does not have this optimism without her prayer. She
doesn't manifest this joy without her rootedness in
her Catholic faith.

Father Jim F. Chamberlain,
speaking about Sister Rosemary Nyirumbe

When Sister Rosemary met Pope Francis in person in
September 2016, she was moved to tears by his kindness.
"I could not say anything but hold his hands," she says, still
amazed at her unlikely loss of words. She handed him a
copy of the *Sewing Hope* book translated in Italian, *Cucire
la Speranza*, and when Pope Francis saw the book cover, a
photo of her with a baby girl wrapped on her back in a
traditional colorful *kitenge* cloth, he smiled his trademark
grin and asked Sister Rosemary, "Is this you?"

"When I responded 'yes,' he gave me a gentle pat on my
left cheek, just as was done when I received my confirma-
tion!" she recalls, and Sister Rosemary, with eyes closed to

take in the fullness of that perfect moment, instinctively raised her left hand and placed it on his, as Pope Francis continued to smile upon her. Sister Rosemary met the pope in Assisi, where she had stopped on a month-long tour to promote the release of the Italian edition. During this time, she traveled throughout the country giving presentations on her work at different religious orders. But the highlight, by far, was meeting Pope Francis. "It was quite emotional for me because I got the sense of Jesus coming physically to touch my hands. That brought tears of joy in my eyes."

Forgiveness: You Can't Give What You Don't Have

When asked to speak a few years ago at the annual diocesan Conference for Catholic Women in Pittsburgh, Sister Rosemary spent a lot of time pondering how to address the topic suggested to her, the role of women in the Year of Mercy. Because of her work with girls at St. Monica's, she decided to focus specifically on forgiveness, mindful of the many levels of forgiveness that her girls had to struggle with—forgiveness of one another, their families, the men who did violence to them, and, ultimately, themselves. Yet her approach, she finally determined, was not only to get in touch with how she lived out forgiveness, but also to give the audience a specific and personal example from her own life.

Not wanting to be dismissed for being a nun, "for *having* to forgive," she stresses, "I took a lot of time to struggle with forgiveness in my own reality. I needed to work through my life and find exactly who I had not forgiven—and what I found out is that I have many people I did not forgive!" Sister Rosemary laughs. Once she did this, it became evident there was one particular orphan whom she needed to forgive first, immediately. "Joseph[1] was someone very close to my heart. I thought I was doing everything to help this boy succeed—and he betrayed me. My reaction was to say, I'm done with him. I'm not doing anything more for him."

Then out of the blue, years later, the boy contacted Sister Rosemary, writing her a letter and asking her to forgive him, even threatening to commit suicide if she said no. "I showed the sisters the letter and I said, 'I'm not forgiving him. If he really wants to commit suicide, he would have done it by now.' I went as far as saying, 'If he commits suicide, we can bury the body.' That's when a friend of mine, one of the sisters, said, 'Rosemary, you have to forgive that boy. Remember the psalm 'If you oh Lord should mark our guilt, who would survive?' (Psalm 130:3). But I felt such hurt, I responded, 'Do not repeat that psalm to me! I am not ready to forgive him.' Saying those words out loud helped me to understand that forgiveness is a journey . . . and I journeyed with it."

Once she received the invitation to talk to women about forgiveness and compassion, "I challenged myself," she confesses. "I knew it was time to forgive this boy. I called him, and I had to act to forgive him. His response was, 'Sister, this is a miracle, that you are talking to me today!' I told Joseph, 'I want you to understand that it is the call to forgiveness in this year of mercy, and I am doing it to you. You do it to others. I want you to know that I'm asking you to do the same, and you'll be closer to God.' That's all the message I gave him," Sister Rosemary says. "He went back to college, which thrilled me. It's something that made me think, how, when we don't forgive you are actually killing a part of yourself, not just someone else. And that's a message for all of us." She stops to emphasize, "It is *hard*! That's the message I shared with the women. I asked, 'How many of you have children that you have not forgiven? How many of you have not forgiven your husbands?' The truth is that we are all afraid of these challenges!"

It is clear that prayer fuels Sister Rosemary's every effort, seeking the Eucharist everywhere she travels. "I am dedicated to my rosary, even if I don't complete it!" she says with a laugh. Also, "I've got a lot of devotion to Our Lady, which is strange because [as a Sacred Heart of Jesus sister] I should have more devotion to His Sacred Heart! But Our Lady gives me answers very fast," she says and then smiles.

Her prayer before the Blessed Sacrament is simple, explains Sister Rosemary, and always rooted in thanksgiving. "My prayer is, '*Lord you are with me, so if I go out in your name, let everyone I meet know that you are with me. I am thankful that you come to me, who is unworthy.*'"

A Eucharistic Discipleship

In his 2018 apostolic exhortation, *Gaudete et Exsultate* (Rejoice and Be Glad): On the Call to Holiness in Today's World,[2] Pope Francis emphasizes that holiness is a call for each of us, without exception: "We are frequently tempted to think that holiness is only for those who can withdraw from ordinary affairs to spend much time in prayer. That is not the case. We are all called to be holy by living our lives with love and by bearing witness in everything we do, wherever we find ourselves" (14). This holiness to which the Lord calls each person will grow through what the pope describes as "small gestures," and how that holiness is lived out is particular to each person. Pope Francis explains, "The important thing is that each believer discern his or her own path, that they bring out the very best of themselves, the most personal gifts that God has placed in their hearts (cf. *1 Cor* 12:7), rather than hopelessly trying to imitate something not meant for them. We are all called to be witnesses, but there are many actual ways of bearing witness" (11).

In a statement remarkably apropos to the work at St. Monica's, Pope Francis could be describing Sister Rosemary and the Sisters of the Sacred Heart of Jesus when he says, "I would stress too that the 'genius of woman' is seen in feminine styles of holiness, which are an essential means of reflecting God's holiness in this world. Indeed, in times when women tended to be most ignored or overlooked, the Holy Spirit raised up saints whose attractiveness produced new spiritual vigour and important reforms in the Church. We can mention Saint Hildegard of Bingen, Saint Bridget, Saint Catherine of Siena, Saint Teresa of Ávila and Saint Thérèse of Lisieux. But I think too of all those unknown or forgotten women who, each in her own way, sustained and transformed families and communities by the power of their witness" (12).

"You too need to see the entirety of your life as a mission," stresses Pope Francis, in words that seem to be describing the ever-changing journey and vocation response of Sister Rosemary and the Sisters of the Sacred Heart of Jesus. "Try to do so by listening to God in prayer and recognizing the signs that he gives you. Always ask the Spirit what Jesus expects from you at every moment of your life and in every decision you must make, so as to discern its place in the mission you have received. Allow the Spirit to forge in you the personal mystery that can reflect Jesus Christ in today's world.

"May you come to realize what that word is, the message of Jesus that God wants to speak to the world by your life. Let yourself be transformed. Let yourself be renewed by the Spirit, so that this can happen, lest you fail in your precious mission. The Lord will bring it to fulfillment despite your mistakes and missteps, provided that you do not abandon the path of love but remain ever open to his supernatural grace, which purifies and enlightens" (23–24).

Pope Francis goes on to point out that, in the Beatitudes, Jesus explains with simplicity what it means to be holy, to seek holiness—what a practical response to living the Gospel looks like:

> Being poor of heart: that is holiness. (70)
> Reacting with meekness and humility: that is holiness. (74)
> Hungering and thirsting for righteousness: that is holiness. (79)
> Seeing and acting with mercy: that is holiness. (82)
> Keeping a heart free of all that tarnishes love: that is holiness. (86)
> Sowing peace all around us: that is holiness. (89)
> Accepting daily the path of the Gospel, even though it may cause us problems: that is holiness. (94)

And finally, in a beatitude response describing particularly well the work of the Sisters of the Sacred Heart of Jesus, "Knowing how to mourn with others: that is holiness," Pope Francis remarks. "A person who sees things as they truly are and sympathizes with pain and sorrow is capable of touching life's depths and finding authentic happiness. He or she is consoled, not by the world but by Jesus. Such persons are unafraid to share in the suffering of others; they do not flee from painful situations. They discover the meaning of life by coming to the aid of those who suffer, understanding their anguish and bringing relief. They sense that the other is flesh of our flesh, and are not afraid to draw near, even to touch their wounds. They feel compassion for others in such a way that all distance vanishes. In this way they can embrace Saint Paul's exhortation: 'Weep with those who weep'" (76).

Life at St. Monica's—and in northern Uganda—has changed a lot since Sister Rosemary took charge of the school in 2001. The community could have never guessed that their ministry to recent returnees would evolve into a holistic care for the person—and for the family a girl brings with her. Or that the vision that first fueled St. Monica's would expand to several different sites in northern Uganda, now serving the refugee women and children from South Sudan with nowhere to go. Yet the sisters have never stopped weeping with those who weep, sowing peace in the region and in each child's heart by living and being the Gospel of presence—and by loving each one right where they are, as they are. To have known this future and what God had in mind for them, agrees Sister Rosemary, would have been detrimental. "I just kept responding to what God put in front of me. Honestly, if you knew the mind of God, it'd be terrible!" she says with a laugh.

For Father Jim F. Chamberlain, a diocesan priest incardinated in Austin, Texas, who has spent a month every summer at St. Monica's since 2016, what gives Sister Rosemary her strength and what drives her vision is quite obvious. "Every time I am there in Gulu for the summer month, Sister Rosemary insists that I celebrate Mass with her and her sisters each day at 7 a.m.," he says, smiling. "The sisters sing and pray and laugh. She's not in a leadership role there but is simply one of the faithful disciples gathered in prayer around the table of the Eucharist.

"I want the world to see this side of her, which is hard to know simply from watching her speak or in viewing a documentary about her life," he underscores. "She prays with the sisters each night before evening meal, and one can hear them praying and singing softly together from the convent's second floor at St. Monica's. That personal prayer life is what I am in most awe about—and about which I would want the world to know." Father Jim, an environmental engineer who works as co-director for Education and Outreach at the University of Oklahoma's WaTER Center,[3] has worked with Sister Rosemary and the sisters each summer traveling to their various campuses in order to establish sustainable water and sanitation projects.

According to Father Jim, there are two things about Sister Rosemary that stand out—her patience and her openness to welcoming the stranger. "It seems that she will not turn anyone away who wants to accompany her on her mission. And she is patient with those who are still learning about that mission, about the challenges she faces," he explains, adding how the emphasis for the sisters' work has changed from girls orphaned and abused by Joseph Kony's army, to now, ministering to many refugees from South Sudan. One of the things he respects most about Sister Rosemary is the fact that she is a "lifelong learner, as evidenced by her desire to pursue a PhD in education. She also spent much of a recent summer in Italy, studying the Italian language. She is constantly curious, and this can be a hindrance in keeping focused on one project, as my OU [University of Oklahoma] colleagues can attest," he says with a laugh. "But such is really a reflection of her continuing desire to learn and to advance her mission for providing care for the orphaned and homeless refugees who are in such need in northern Uganda."

On one of her recent trips to the United States, Sister Rosemary made a point of traveling to Father Jim's small rural parish in Purcell, Oklahoma, to meet him at his home—like he has met Sister Rosemary at hers—and to give a reflection at Mass one Sunday morning. "She really impressed my parishioners," says Father Jim, emphasizing that the 385 families of Our Lady of Victory Catholic Church had never met someone like Sister Rosemary. "I am proud of our friendship and of the fact that she is willing to spend valuable time with me and with my parishioners."

The first adjectives describing Sister Rosemary have to be "optimistic and full of joy!" Father Jim notes. "I have never seen her when she was more than moments away from a huge smile, a smile of optimism. Even when we are talking about things that are serious, she manifests such an optimistic spirit of 'Yes, we can. We can do this! We have to do this!' She often thinks out loud, what engineers call 'brainstorming,' about new ideas that she has for her orphanages or clinics or the communities or sisters." But perhaps what impresses him the most is that, as she talks about them, "They become real imagined possibilities because they are always undergirded with that ever-present optimism!" According to Father Jim, being optimistic and full of joy are intrinsically connected, because, "Someone can only afford to be joyful who has that much optimism. It is the same kind of joy that must have been felt by the first disciples after the resurrection and outpouring of the Holy Spirit. There is nothing that they could not now do, undergirded by the confidence that they felt in the risen Christ."

Work Diligently and with Love

Sister Rosemary sits on a plastic chair on the red dirt under a mango tree, looking for shade. Three roosters above her start crowing, each hanging on a different tree limb, as if announcing Sister Rosemary's arrival to the 100-acre Sewing Hope Children's Village in Atiak. Nearby, one of the kindergarten classes prepares to come sing to her, lining up two by two to cross the field to where Sister Rosemary awaits. A few moments after Sister sits down, a woman in her twenties seems to come out of nowhere to talk to Sister, kneeling in front of her. They have a short, pleasant conversation in the woman's native language before Sister Rosemary pulls out her phone and shows her a few photos; then the woman places her hand on her chest and, with tears in her eyes, says with emotion, "That is so good!"

"We removed five kids from her," explains Sister Rosemary. The woman pulls out and gives medical papers to update Sister Rosemary on her condition, being HIV positive. "Three of the children are here. Two of them, five-year-old twins, are living in Spain with adoptive parents. They speak Spanish now," Sister Rosemary emphasizes, pointing to the photos that she was showing the young woman. "They were so malnourished when we found them! And she was struggling to survive. . . . But she is doing so well now," Sister Rosemary says, smiling at the woman once again. "I'm going to take her picture and send it to [the twins] to show them!"

At their village in Atiak, which originally began as a second vocational school, the sisters now provide a school open to all the kids in the area. There is also an orphanage divided into "houses" with a "mother" assigned to each home and with a playground to be shared by all the children. The vision is Sister Rosemary's, who notes that the child-to-caretaker ratio is meant to be eight to one, with each small group living in individual homes. "We don't want them to feel like orphans here, but part of a family," she explains, adding that the unique arrangement makes their caregiving practical, but also ministers to the children's unique needs. "The whole idea is for these kids to grow as normal children," with every aspect of the plans working together, in fact, to make it one whole—ever growing—village of many programs. The teenage girls

old enough to take sewing classes in their vocational programs serve as models, even mentors, to the fifty-something
younger students and orphans who live and attend school on
the other side of the school compound.

After listening with delight to several songs chanted and
sung by the kindergarten students, Sister Rosemary gets up
and walks to the other side of the two round huts, one a
chapel served by a small solar panel near its entrance, and
the other serving as the sisters' living quarters. In a cleared
area with red-dirt floor, Sister Rosemary sits down in a circle
of chairs that have been arranged under a large makeshift
canopy made of poles and plastic sheets. She begins addressing a group of contractors, five men and one woman, who
have come to a meeting to discuss with Sister Rosemary the
construction they are about to undertake—two new buildings, including a new dispensary.

"Remember the sisters are here with you. You need to
show them respect," Sister Rosemary begins, and everyone
nods. "The sisters are the key to whatever we are doing. I
have great sisters who bring their strengths to this work.

"The most important thing is timely reports," she remarks, before explaining what she means. "If we want
people who are supporting us to give us the funding [we
need], we have to give them timely reports. We have to be
respectful of them. We know how difficult it is to get money!
So whatever you do, whatever you build, do it right." Sister
Rosemary pauses to look at each face. "What is your con-
tribution to what you're doing? Have pride in it. We want
things to be built in a way that will last for us. What we are
building here is not for me, it's not for any sisters, it's not
for Mario," she says, looking over at the project manager,
"it's for all of us, it's for your grandchildren! Make sure you
work together. Work diligently and, always, with love."

Mario then takes over the discussion, addressing each of the people gathered there and their specific goals on the upcoming construction. "We work as a team. We are not supposed to each do things and leave things for others," he says, nodding his head. "We do everything for the betterment of the project."

"Also take excellent care of this machine!" Sister Rosemary chimes in, pointing to the brick-making machine that will make their work possible. "You know how much I struggled to get this machine for years! It's a $47,000 machine. You are the first caretakers of this machine. Please take care of this machine, very, very seriously. . . . Don't make me cry on that one—or have to come here and scream like an African woman!" she jokes, keeping her face serious while making everyone in the circle laugh out loud.

Gladys, the project engineer, takes a turn addressing the group. "I thank you for this opportunity," she begins, looking at the men around her. "I will expect much from you. If we don't know something, it's better to say, 'My brother, can you help me?' I will use you much. I pray we should all be open." Then turning to Sister Rosemary, Gladys emphasizes, "As a mother, I'll try my best to mother them as we go along. We will do our best, Sister. I promise you that. Thank you for your motherly time for us!" Everyone stands and with a small bow showing respect, each person takes a turn shaking Sister Rosemary's hand, as she beams with joy.

The Atiak campus—with seventy-five women and forty children—is so close to the South Sudan border that it now has a considerable number of children in the orphanage from South Sudan, as well as girls who are in Atiak as refugees. "That's why I call it Sewing Hope Children's Village. You get children living together with a 'mom,' or maybe two mothers, to help take care of them; it's more than a regular orphanage." There are a lot of regulations that Sister Rosemary insists they need to follow as their vision continues to grow, but "We are following them as we set up with the children slowly." The first of the "home" buildings was built by the US athletes (Pros for Africa), and it is still in use. Sister Rosemary named one of the new buildings at Atiak the Brandon Whitten Hall, in recognition and remembrance of the son of their benefactor, Reggie Whitten, another blessing born out of tragedy. A recently installed water well provides them with fresh water, thanks to Father Jim Chamberlain and the University of Oklahoma's WaTER Center project. As is true in most of Uganda, small solar panels outside every building and hut serve as a limited source of electricity.

Because they have so many refugees fleeing the violence in South Sudan, notes Sister Doreen Oyella, the sister in charge of the Atiak campus, the United Nations wants the school to build "a wall for security," reminiscent of the numerous refugee camps that currently dot the entire Ugandan border region. "The refugees are from different districts, different tribes, speaking different languages. Many of (the South Sudan) refugees speak Arabic and have to learn English to communicate with the people here in Uganda."

But Sewing Hope Children's Village, like so much that the Sisters of the Sacred Heart community does, is a much bigger vision—with ultimately a different purpose. Its residents cross tribal divisions, with "many languages spoken—Madi, Acholi, Alur," notes Sister Doreen. "Our ability as sisters to speak many languages has been very powerful here." In addition to education for children and older girls, the residents are also growing gardens for their food, and they are recipients of the sisters' unconditional love for each of them, regardless of their past or wrongdoings.

"Our presence here has brought many changes, maybe not in a mighty way. But even the fact that people are also coming to settle near us, near the village, that's also a positive thing," says Sister Rosemary. "When our community first came, there were no people here left to help. No dispensary, nothing. Slowly people started coming; now they are here Friday night to be here for Saturday morning dispensary. I don't think for our sisters there would have been a better location in Uganda, near the border, than Atiak," she stresses, noting that Sewing Hope Children's Village is four hours south, all tarmac, of Juba, South Sudan, where their mother-house is located. Traveling to Juba from the village, she points out, is closer than traveling from Atiak to Kampala, the Ugandan capital.

Who Is My Brother?

Sister Rosemary sits at the dining table of her convent home in Gulu, answering emails from an Italian journalist. One of her sisters walks into the room and sits near her, bringing both of them a drink for teatime—a British custom that they still practice. But Sister Assumpta actually drinks tea, while Sister Rosemary drinks coffee, her favorite drink. "How are exams, hard?" Sister Rosemary asks Sister Assumpta. "What was today?" The sister responds in a blend of her native language and English. In addition to the 250 women that Sister Assumpta works with, there are 150 children attending St. Monica's kindergarten and daycare center.

Because the need for a kindergarten and daycare center at St. Monica's grew very rapidly, decisions had to be made on the spot. At one point, Sister Rosemary remembers, they had several of Kony's children at the school—a fact both mothers and sisters wanted to keep hidden, for the safety of the children. But this fact also became a symbol of healing, as the center opened up to children outside St. Monica's as a source of income for the school. That children of the rebels were mingling daily with the children from Gulu was a model not lost on Sister Rosemary.

As Sister Rosemary takes a sip of her aromatic coffee, a tall young man walks into the room and Sister Rosemary stops what she's doing to look straight at him.

"Sister, I've come to seek your permission," Patrick says, with downcast eyes. "I want to buy cooking oil."

Without waiting a beat, Sister Rosemary begins by requesting that he look up at her and then directs him to greet everyone in the room properly before she responds to his request.

"Patrick, what did you buy yesterday?"

"A packet of flour."

"And the day before?"

"Sugar," he responds shyly.

"When you want to do something like this, make a plan. Don't just write down what you buy each day. No, write all the things you need down, one, two, three, four, five—and go buy them all. Now go; write it down and bring it to me, okay? Thank you, Patrick."

Abandoned by his parents in Atiak, Patrick was so swollen from malnutrition that the other kids used to call him monkey, says Sister Rosemary. The sisters took him to Adjumani, where he did very well at the primary school. "He's good at every subject," Sister Rosemary says, smiling proudly. "He was the second best in his district." She speaks about each child with the same loving pride that a mother talks to her friends about her children, listing his or her accomplishments and their special talents and traits.

"Patrick is now in the vocational school. He's learning how to cook. He makes donuts every day and sells them. But we have to be patient with him!" exclaims Sister Rosemary, noting that his stature makes him look much older than his thirteen years of age. "He is very smart. I gave him a book of accounts and he's learning to write it all out. I want him to know as he goes back to school just how well he's working!

"He wrote a very beautiful letter for me," Sister Rosemary continues, getting up to look for the letter. "It's in his own handwriting, saying things like, 'Sister, I will never forget you because you took me in when my own mother abandoned me.'. . . I could not believe this letter! He wrote three envelopes, marked with 'May God bless you abundantly!'" she says, laughing loudly. "It took me so long to teach this boy to even look at people. Every time he would turn his back, I'd have to tell him, greet and look at people!"

As soon as Patrick enters the room again, notebook in hand, Sister Rosemary stops smiling and puts on her serious face and tone of voice—an echo of her own years as a novice when the mother superior took special attention to notice and encourage her.

"Things to be bought," Patrick says, showing her the list, "five liters of cooking oil. One sack of flour . . ."

Sister Rosemary listens to all of it and then patiently replies, "How much money do you have? How much more money do you need? What about transport, Patrick? List everything. I want to see your whole book of accounts. Don't ask me for things one by one."

As soon as he leaves the room, Sister Rosemary laughs again, prompting one of the other sisters to say, "You are patient! I am not that patient!"

A True Missionary Disciple

Long before Pope Francis called on Catholic laity to become "missionary disciples," Sister Rosemary and the Sisters of the Sacred Heart of Jesus had been living and ministering their vocation as true apostles of the Word and in the world. Filled with his spirit, they have directly touched the lives of thousands in Uganda, Kenya, and South Sudan, becoming the living face of Christ for some of the most hurting people in the world today. It is not a coincidence that there are only two areas in the world where vocations to religious life among Catholic women are growing rather than declining—one is Africa and the other is Asia.

In Uganda alone, between 2005 and 2015, the number of women religious grew an impressive 26 percent—not a minor fact in a country where thousands died in the tribal wars and genocide.[4] With their motherhouse in Juba, South Sudan, the Sisters of the Sacred Heart are no exception. The community has over 250 women religious living out their motto—"Live Love in Truth"—in South Sudan, Kenya, and Uganda, where most Sacred Heart vocations come from. "I think the girls look at what we are doing and they are attracted to it; they want to be a part of it. Every year St. Monica sends girls to the convent."

Education, Sister Rosemary emphasizes, is non-negotiable for any girl entering the convent. "We send the girls back to school if they have not had formal education. It is very important to have girls educated in order for them to be able to meet the challenges of the world tomorrow," she says. After pausing, she then adds, "I met a congregation in Uganda where some of the sisters are not educated. I was shocked! I think this is quite unjust, because they will not be able to as missionaries accomplish as much. If you don't have the language to communicate with people, you're not going to know their problems. You won't be effective in your ministry. I offered these sisters to come and join our girl literacy program. We can teach them to read and write."

It is ironic that a notable part of Sister Rosemary's work now is speaking at functions and meeting with dignitaries. "I don't see a difference between what I do in Gulu and what I do when I travel, although the jet lag reminds me that I'm in a different world!" she jokes during an interview at the Pros for Africa office in Oklahoma City. "Yesterday I was in Texas. Today I got an email from a prince and princess in Yugoslavia. Later this week I'll be in New York. The people I meet I see as human beings. I don't see a lot of difference. I think God really wants all of us to be equal, to treat each other the same, no one better or higher. We are the same. And as Catholics it is very important that our message be how much God really loves us, that no one is less. I'm beginning to see this more and more."

Facing evil may look different because of other cultures, notes Sister Rosemary, but perhaps what makes what happened in Uganda incalculable is "the magnitude of it, especially the aftermath. Now you can see how the war has impacted very, very negatively on people for a long time. . . . It's like it has thrown our people back in that part of northern Uganda to almost like the Stone Age. . . . I now totally believe not everyone knows what has happened with us. That's why we need to open our eyes, go beyond our world to find out what's happening elsewhere, because the suffering of someone, even in Africa, it's the same. We are walking the same path."

One of the perspectives that Sister Rosemary says she has gained thanks to her participation in international conferences and presentations is an understanding that some problems are universal. At a recent international conference in Dallas, for example, where Sister Rosemary spoke about the sisters' work at St. Monica's helping mothers to love their own children who were not expected (from their lives in the bush), someone in the audience stood up and said, "A friend's daughter is sixteen years old and she's expecting a baby but they could not get a legal abortion." To this, Sister Rosemary replied, "I wish they spoke to me. I would have told them, 'Give the children to me! I will take care of them'! You see, it is the same problem that I had here."

The Message Remains: You Can't Sugarcoat Evil

Speaking to several hundred Catholic journalists at the annual Catholic Media Conference in Buffalo a few years ago, Sister Rosemary described to the captivated audience the daily challenges of helping women who are still suffering from the wounds of violence, women whom the world has forgotten about. She urged the media editors, reporters, and publishers to tell the story of the children in northern Uganda, to talk about what happened there, as detailed in the documentary *Sewing Hope*, concluding with the words, "You can't sugarcoat evil. As Catholics we can show our faith by taking the lead. Please, tell the stories. It is not old news!"

According to the United Nations, child abductions in Africa continue. The UN's child protection team notes, for example, that intertribal abductions are on the rise in South Sudan, where a child is worth twenty cows or about $7,000. In Nigeria, western Africa, Boko Haram's abductions of schoolgirls led to the international battle cry #BringbackourGirls—yet four years later, over one hundred of those girls are still missing.

Of course, the situation is different in northern Uganda, where the active abductions of children ended in 2006. Yet the girls escaping from bush captivity continue, even now. "Just last year we had girls who came to us from captivity," Sister Rosemary exclaims. "There was one who stayed with the rebels for nine years, then came to us at our school in Atiak. It was so hard to even connect with the feelings of this girl. She had no emotion. She kept saying, 'Sister, I've been with the rebels all these years—I don't know if I can learn.' I just said, 'Yes, you can learn!' Then she'd say, 'No one cares about me.' And we'd say over and over, 'Estella, we care about you.' We gave her a chance and she came to St. Monica's for one year. I'm hopeful we can give her an education in seamstressing. This year we have two girls who came to us who were BORN in captivity!"

Although normally the sisters like to distribute the work evenly among the girls, to help them support their families, Sister Rosemary admits that each case is different. One girl named Beatrice,[5] for example, "has five children from captivity and she's thirty-two. You can still see the line of pain in her face, the line of suffering." She adds, "For this girl, I make sure she makes as many purses or shirts as she wants, because the more she makes, the more money I can give her to take care of those children."

So while appearances make life in Uganda seem normal, in reality, says Sister Rosemary, "Uganda is going to be recovering from this for a long time. My effort, right now, is to not let the world forget this situation. I cannot let everyone forget that people here continue to suffer. They can't possibly just recover in a year or two. We have to be there for them, in different ways, to let the girls know that the world still cares about them." It is essential that the work continues, emphasizes Sister Rosemary, because "every time we tell the story, read the book [*Sewing Hope*], watch this movie . . . we are putting in effort to try to stop this evil from happening again."

Across the Atlantic, the Sewing Hope Foundation is now carrying on the original mission of Pros for Africa, coordinating Sister Rosemary's visits and invitations to speak. "Meeting more people helps retell the story!" explains Sister Rosemary. And the Pros for Africa initiative has evolved into the development partner that supports Sister Rosemary by encouraging and assisting universities, colleges, students, and professors of all fields to volunteer in her work as she fights to educate and support the victimized—especially women and children. The "pros" enlisted by Pros for Africa include physicians, nurses, attorneys, engineers, designers, carpenters, educators, entrepreneurs, and medical and law students. "It turns out that Pros for Africa is best run by students and faculty from different universities, which makes sense because they keep on passing it from one student to another and so it keeps spreading," Sister Rosemary says. "It has become a big machine, getting students to come and work as volunteers. It is wonderful that many come back or continue supporting the work in one way or another. They become part of the mission!"

Sister Rosemary and the Sisters of the Sacred Heart of Jesus currently serve at their two schools, one in Gulu and the other in Atiak, Uganda, with a third school under construction in Torit, South Sudan.

If there had not been a Reggie Whitten connection, if he had not been brought to Uganda by his dear friends, if he had not been to Uganda and met Sister Rosemary, would no one outside Africa have heard about her and her work? "Perhaps," acknowledges Sister Rosemary. "Perhaps our story would have been known in a different way, at a different time. Yet it is Divine Providence that they picked that time, a difficult time in my life, at a difficult moment" to come. "How else do you explain that?"

Regardless of how it happened, Sister Rosemary and her community continue to live and to witness for the rest of the world what Pope Francis calls "the middle class of holiness." This is what, paraphrasing *Lumen Gentium*, Pope Francis describes as "the signs of holiness that the Lord shows us through the humblest members of that people which 'shares also in Christ's prophetic office, spreading abroad a living witness to him, especially by means of a life of faith and charity.'"[6]

As far as the future is concerned, the only thing Sister Rosemary feels certain about is more of a wish. "When I get old I want a place where I can come and still be useful, perhaps teach the girls," she says, grinning, then laughs, "But I need to be around children!"

Notes

Introduction—pages 1–9

1. Not her real name.

Chapter One:
Little Sister's Beginnings (1956–1975)—
pages 11–29

1. Republic of Uganda, "Education in Uganda," Ministry of Education and Sports, http://www.education.go.ug/data/smenu/43/Education+in+Uganda.html.

2. Office of the Prime Minister, "Facts & Figures," Government of Uganda, http://gou.go.ug/about-uganda/sector/facts-figures.

3. Reggie Whitten and Nancy Henderson, *Sewing Hope* (Oklahoma City: Dust Jacket Press, 2013), 129.

4. Kathleen Jones, ed., "June 3 SS Charles Lwanga and Companions," in *Butler's Lives of the Saints* (Collegeville, MN: Liturgical Press, 1997), 22–24.

5. Raimundo Rocha, "Comboni Missionaries in South Sudan Celebrate 150 Years of Foundation of Their Missionary Institute," June 9, 2017, http://combonisouthsudan.org/comboni-missionaries-in-south-sudan-celebrate-150-years-of-foundation-of-their-missionary-institute/.

6. Pew Research Center, *Global Christianity*, December 1, 2014, http://www.pewforum.org/interactives/global-christianity/#/Uganda,Catholic.

7. CARA, *Global Catholicism: Trends & Forecasts*, June 4, 2015, 25, https://cara.georgetown.edu/staff/webpages/Global%20Catholicism%20Release.pdf.

8. Conor Gaffey, "Jesus Has Found a Home Here: The Rise of Catholicism in Africa," *Newsweek*, November 30, 2015, http://www.newsweek.com/jesus-has-found-home-here-rise-catholicism-africa-399114.

9. Patrick Keatley, "Idi Amin: Obituary," *The Guardian*, US Edition, August 17, 2003, https://www.theguardian.com/news/2003/aug/18/guardianobituaries.

10. "Idi Amin," *Wikipedia*, https://en.wikipedia.org/wiki/Idi_Amin.

Chapter Two:
A Comboni Spirituality (1976–1986)—pages 30–43

1. Anthony Low, "The British and the Baganda," *International Affairs (Royal Institute of International Affairs 1944–)* 32, no. 3 (1956): 308–17, https://www.jstor.org/stable/2608109.

2. "Uganda Profile—Timeline," *BBC News*, May 10, 2018, http://www.bbc.com/news/world-africa-14112446.

3. George Thomas Kurian, "Uganda—Ethnic Groups," *Encyclopedia of the Third World*, 4th ed., vol. 3 (New York: Facts on File, 1992), https://www.africa.upenn.edu/NEH/u-ethn.html.

4. "St. Mary's Midwifery Training School: To Love and Serve with Joy," http://www.kalongomidwifery.org/index.html.

5. Amnesty International, "Uganda: The Human Rights Record 1986–1989," Amnesty International Publications (March 1989), 7, https://www.amnesty.org/en/documents/afr59/001/1989/en/.

6. "Daniel Comboni (1831–1881)," The Holy See, http://www.vatican.va/news_services/liturgy/saints/ns_lit_doc_20031005_comboni_en.html.

Chapter Three:
Little Things with Great Love (1987–2000)—
pages 44–61

1. Louis Jadwong, "Yoweri Museveni Swears in January 29, 1986," https://youtu.be/aZRflYMxEGY.

2. Robert Gersony, "The Anguish of Northern Uganda: Results of a Field-Based Assessment of the Civil Conflicts in Northern Uganda," USAID Mission to Kampala, October 2, 1997, 24, https://reliefweb.int/report/uganda/anguish-northern-uganda-introduction.

3. "Sacred Heart SS Remains a Beacon of Hope in the North," *New Vision*, November 4, 2001, https://www.newvision.co.ug/print _article/new_vision/news/1022525/sacred-heart-ss-remains-beacon -hope-north?print=true.

4. Gersony, "The Anguish of Northern Uganda," 30.

5. David Lean, dir., *The Bridge on the River Kwai* (Los Angeles: Columbia Pictures, 1957).

6. Reggie Whitten and Nancy Henderson, *Sewing Hope* (Oklahoma City: Dust Jacket Press, 2013), 60.

7. Donald H. Dunson, *No Room at the Table: Earth's Most Vulnerable Children* (Maryknoll, NY: Orbis Books, 2003), 13–14, 28, 16.

8. Gary Smith, "Child Soldiers and the Lord's Resistance Army," *America*, March 29, 2004, https://www.americamagazine.org /issue/479/article/child-soldiers-and-lords-resistance-army.

9. Amnesty International, "Uganda: The Human Rights Record 1986–1989," Amnesty International Publications, March 1989, 1, https://www.amnesty.org/en/documents/afr59/001/1989/en/.

10. Gersony, "The Anguish of Northern Uganda," 33.

11. Sebhat Ayele, "Pope John Paul II Visit to Uganda in 1993," *Leadership*, September 1, 2015, http://leadershipmagazine.org/?p =7284.

12. Gulu Archdiocese, News, http://www.archdioceseofgulu.org /update/JPIIVisit.htm.

13. Gulu Archdiocese, "Let My People Go: The Forgotten Plight of the People in the Displaced Camps in Acholi" (July 2001): 8.

14. Ibid., 9.

15. Ali B. Ali-Dinar, ed., "Humanitarian Situation Report on Uganda," United Nations Department of Humanitarian Affairs, University of Pennsylvania African Studies Center, March 15, 1997, http://www.africa.upenn.edu/Hornet/irin_31597.html.

Chapter Four:
With a Motherly Heart (2001–2007)—
pages 62–84

1. Ali B. Ali-Dinar, ed., "Humanitarian Situation Report on Uganda," United Nations Department of Humanitarian Affairs, University of Pennsylvania African Studies Center, March 15, 1997, no. 13, http://www.africa.upenn.edu/Hornet/irin_31597.html.

2. Jeevan Vasagar, "The Nightwalkers," *The Guardian*, February 9, 2006, https://www.theguardian.com/world/2006/feb/10/uganda.jeevanvasagar.

3. Not her real name.

4. Melanie Lidman, "African Tradition Blends with Religion to Illuminate Path to Forgiveness," *Global Sisters Report*, November 19, 2014, https://www.globalsistersreport.org/african-tradition-blends-religion-illuminate-path-forgiveness-15136.

5. Reggie Whitten and Nancy Henderson, *Sewing Hope* (Oklahoma City: Dust Jacket Press, 2013), 93.

6. Donald H. Dunson, *No Room at the Table: Earth's Most Vulnerable Children* (Maryknoll, NY: Orbis Books, 2003), 15.

7. Ibid., 34.

8. Ibid., 35.

9. Not her real name.

10. Whitten and Henderson, *Sewing Hope*, 4–5.

11. Ibid., 164.

12. Sister Rosemary Nyirumbe, "Acceptance Address for CNN Heroes Community Crusader Award," American Rhetoric Online Speech Bank, December 9, 2007, http://www.americanrhetoric.com/mp3clips/speeches/sisterrosemarynyirumbecnnheroes.mp3.

Chapter Five:
Love Is the Key! (2008–2017)—pages 85–106

1. Patricia Smith, "Crossing the River Nile with CNN Hero 2007—Sister Rosemary Nyirumbe," My Hero, July 3, 2014, http://ireport.cnn.com/docs/DOC-1106426.

2. Reggie Whitten and Nancy Henderson, *Sewing Hope* (Oklahoma City: Dust Jacket Press, 2013), 142–43.

3. Ibid., 123–24.

4. "Lord's Resistance Army Disarmament and Northern Uganda Recovery Act of 2009," GovTrack, August 25, 2010, https://www.govtrack.us/congress/bills/111/s1067/text.

5. Yon Yamamoto, "The Deployment of U.S. Forces in Central Africa and Implementation of the Lord's Resistance Army Disarmament and Northern Uganda Recovery Act of 2009," U.S. Department of State, Testimony before the House Foreign Affairs Committee, October 25, 2011, https://2009-2017.state.gov/p/af/rls/rm/2011/176160.htm.

6. "UNHCR Closes Chapter on Uganda's Internally Displaced People," UNHCR, January 6, 2012, http://www.unhcr.org/en-us/news/briefing/2012/1/4f06e2a79/unhcr-closes-chapter-ugandas-internally-displaced-people.html.

7. Whitten and Henderson, *Sewing Hope*, 174.

8. Ibid., 133.

9. Whitten and Henderson, *Sewing Hope*, 229–30.

10. Belinda Luscombe, "This Nun's Incredible Speech Wowed a Roomful of VIPs," *Time*, April 30, 2014, http://time.com/82606/sister-rosemary-nyirumbe-time100/.

11. *The Colbert Report*, "#BringbackourGirls—Rosemary Nyirumbe," May 13, 2014, http://www.cc.com/video-clips/2rgt3x/the-colbert-report--bringbackourgirls---rosemary-nyirumbe.

12. "Sister Rosemary vs Stephen Colbert," September 9, 2014, https://www.youtube.com/watch?v=CTGwtCsI0Wk.

13. "The Malopolskie Voivodeship Award of John Paul II Veritatis Splendor 2016 went to Sister Rosemary Nyirumbe," Województwo Małopolskie, 2016, http://nagrodaveritatissplendor.pl/index.php/en/winners/35-sister-rosemary-nyirumbe.

Chapter Six:
The Genius of Woman (2018–)—pages 107–28

1. Not his real name.

2. Pope Francis, *Gaudete et Exsultate*, March 19, 2018, http://w2.vatican.va/content/francesco/en/apost_exhortations/documents/papa-francesco_esortazione-ap_20180319_gaudete-et-exsultate.html.

3. Gallogly College of Engineering Water Center, The University of Oklahoma, http://www.ou.edu/coe/centers/water/people/faculty.

4. Bibiana M. Ngundo and Jonathon Wiggins, *Women Religious in Africa*, CARA Special Report, Summer 2017, https://cara.georgetown.edu/AfricanSisters2017.pdf.

5. Not her real name.

6. *Lumen Gentium* 12, quoted in Pope Francis, *Gaudete et Exsultate* 8.

Bibliography

Print

Brown, Camille Lewis. "African Saints, African Stories: 40 Holy Men and Women." Cincinnati, Ohio: Servant Books, 2008.

Dunson, Donald H. *Child, Victim, Soldier: The Loss of Innocence in Uganda*. Maryknoll, NY: Orbis Books, 2008.

————. *No Room at the Table: Earth's Most Vulnerable Children*. Maryknoll, NY: Orbis Books, 2003.

Gelber, L., and Michael Linssen, OCD. *The Collected Works of Edith Stein: The Hidden Life*. Translated by Waltraut Stein. Washington, DC: ICS Publications, 1992.

Harp, Anne Barajas. "The Lessons of Sister Rosemary." *Sooner Magazine* (Spring 2017).

Hubbard, Jennifer. "Pentecost Sunday." *Magnificat* 20, no. 3 (May 2018).

Jones, Kathleen, ed. "June 3 SS Charles Lwanga and Companions." In *Butler's Lives of the Saints*. Collegeville, MN: Liturgical Press, 1997.

McDonnell, Faith J. H., and Grace Akallo. *Girl Soldier: A Story of Hope for Northern Uganda's Children*. Grand Rapids, MI: Chosen, 2007.

Okumu, Joseph. "Paimol Martyrs." *Leadership* (October 2017).

Pope Francis. *Gaudete et Exsultate* (Rejoice and Be Glad). Vatican City: Libreria Editrice Vaticana, 2018.

Whitten, Reggie, and Nancy Henderson. *Sewing Hope*. Oklahoma City: Dust Jacket Press, 2013.

Online

"#BringBackourGirls—Rosemary Nyirumbe." *The Colbert Report.* May 13, 2014. http://www.cc.com/video-clips/2rgt3x/the -colbert-report--bringbackourgirls---rosemary-nyirumbe.

"Address of His Holiness Benedict XVI to H. E. Mr. Francis K. Butagira New Ambassador of the Republic of Uganda to the Holy See." *L'Osservatore Romano.* December 18, 2009. Vatican.va.

Ali-Dinar, Ali B., ed. "Humanitarian Situation Report on Uganda." United Nations Department of Humanitarian Affairs. University of Pennsylvania African Studies Center. March 15, 1997. http://www.africa.upenn.edu/Hornet/irin_31597 .html.

Amnesty International. "Uganda: The Human Rights Record 1986–1989." Amnesty International Publications. March 1989. https://www.amnesty.org/en/documents/afr59/001 /1989/en/.

Angulibo, Ahmed. "Adjumani Captives Released." *New Vision.* June 30, 2003. https://www.newvision.co.ug/new_vision /news/1265233/adjumani-captives-released.

Ayele, MCCJ, Sebhat. "Pope John Paul II Visit to Uganda in 1993." *Leadership.* September 1, 2015. http://leadershipmagazine .org/?p=7284.

Bordoni, Linda. "Pope Francis Expresses Closeness to South Sudan Ecumenical Delegation." *Vatican News.* March 23, 2018. https://www.vaticannews.va/en/church/news/2018-03 /south-sudan-pope-francis-sant-egidio.html.

CARA (Center for Applied Research in the Apostolate). "Global Catholicism: Trends & Forecasts." June 4, 2015. https:// cara.georgetown.edu/staff/webpages/Global%20 Catholicism%20Release.pdf.

Gaffey, Conor. "Jesus Has Found a Home Here: The Rise of Catholicism in Africa." *Newsweek*. November 30, 2015. http://www.newsweek.com/jesus-has-found-home-here -rise-catholicism-africa-399114.

Gersony, Robert. "The Anguish of Northern Uganda: Results of a Field-Based Assessment of the Civil Conflicts in Northern Uganda." USAID Mission to Kampala. October 2, 1997. https://reliefweb.int/report/uganda/anguish-northern -uganda-introduction.

Gulu Archdiocese. "Let My People Go: The Forgotten Plight of the People in the Displaced Camps in Acholi." July 2001.

Jadwong, Louis. "Yoweri Museveni Swears in January 29, 1986." https://youtu.be/aZRflYMxEGY.

Keatley, Patrick. "Idi Amin: Obituary." *The Guardian*, US Edition. August 17, 2003. https://www.theguardian.com/news /2003/aug/18/guardianobituaries.

Kurian, George Thomas. "Uganda—Ethnic Groups." *Encyclopedia of the Third World*. 4th ed. Vol. 3. New York: Facts on File, 1992. https://www.africa.upenn.edu/NEH/u-ethn .html.

La Salandra, MCCJ, Toni. "The History of the Catholic Church in West Nile." Google Online Index. May 14, 1979.

Lidman, Melanie. "African Tradition Blends with Religion to Illuminate Path to Forgiveness." *Global Sisters Report*. November 19, 2014. https://www.globalsistersreport.org /african-tradition-blends-religion-illuminate-path-forgiveness -15136.

———. "Heart of Forgiveness: Ugandan Women Once Child Soldiers Now Lead Peace." *Global Sisters Report*. December 31, 2017. https://www.globalsistersreport.org/news/equality /heart-forgiveness-ugandan-women-once-child-soldiers -now-lead-peace-51061.

"Lord's Resistance Army Disarmament and Northern Uganda Recovery Act of 2009." GovTrack. August 25, 2010. https://www.govtrack.us/congress/bills/111/s1067/text.

Low, Anthony. "The British and the Baganda." *International Affairs (Royal Institute of International Affairs 1944–)* 32, no. 3 (1956). https://www.jstor.org/stable/2608109.

Luscombe, Belinda. "This Nun's Incredible Speech Wowed a Roomful of VIPs." *Time*. April 30, 2014. http://time.com /82606/sister-rosemary-nyirumbe-time100/.

"The Mother Teresa of Africa: Sr. Rosemary Nyirumbe." *Rome Reports*. January 21, 2017. https://www.romereports.com /en/2017/01/21/the-mother-teresa-of-africa-sr-rosemary -nyirumbe/.

Ngundo, Bibiana M., and Jonathon Wiggins. "Women Religious in Africa." CARA Special Report. Summer 2017. https:// cara.georgetown.edu/AfricanSisters2017.pdf.

Nyirumbe, Rosemary. "Acceptance Address for CNN Heroes Community Crusader Award." American Rhetoric Online Speech Bank. http://www.americanrhetoric.com/mp3clips /speeches/sisterrosemarynyirumbecnnheroes.mp3.

Okiror, Samuel. "End of Joseph Kony Hunt Raises Fears Lord's Resistance Army Could Return." *The Guardian*. May 1, 2017. https://www.theguardian.com/global-development /2017/may/01/end-joseph-kony-hunt-fears-lords-resistance -army-return.

Pew Research Center. *Global Christianity*. Religion & Public Life. December 1, 2014. http://www.pewforum.org/interactives /global-christianity/#/Uganda,Catholic.

Rocha, Raimundo. "Comboni Missionaries in South Sudan Celebrate 150 Years of Foundation of Their Missionary Institute." June 9, 2017. http://combonisouthsudan.org/comboni -missionaries-in-south-sudan-celebrate-150-years-of -foundation-of-their-missionary-institute/.

San Martín, Inés. "Ugandan Nun Aims to Save the World, One Person at a Time." *Crux*. October 5, 2016. https:// cruxnow.com/global-church/2016/10/05/ugandan-nun -aims-save-world-one-person-time/.

"Sister Rosemary vs. Stephen Colbert." September 9, 2014. https:// www.youtube.com/watch?v=CTGwtCsI0Wk.

Smith, Gary. "Child Soldiers and the Lord's Resistance Army." *America*. March 29, 2004. https://www.americamagazine .org/issue/479/article/child-soldiers-and-lords-resistance -army.

Smith, Patricia. "Crossing the River Nile with CNN Hero 2007— Sister Rosemary Nyirumbe." My Hero. July 3, 2014. http://ireport.cnn.com/docs/DOC-1106426.

Vasagar, Jeevan. "The Nightwalkers." *The Guardian*. February 9, 2006. https://www.theguardian.com/world/2006/feb/10 /uganda.jeevanvasagar.

Yamamoto, Yon. "The Deployment of U.S. Forces in Central Africa and Implementation of the Lord's Resistance Army Disarmament and Northern Uganda Recovery Act of 2009." U.S. Department of State. Testimony before the House Foreign Affairs Committee. October 25, 2011. https://2009 -2017.state.gov/p/af/rls/rm/2011/176160.htm.

Index